I0622560

TERESA COLLINS

The House of Hyenas

Dare to gather as a hyena
in a sistership of strength.
Understand your world
and become unmesswithable.

The House of Hyenas
Copyright © 2024 Teresa Collins

Cover design by Jessica Bell
Interior design by Amie McCracken

No part of this book is a substitute for professional medical assistance or accredited mental health counselling. Every community has an emergency service which can be instantly accessed for immediate help and should be in the case of a medical or mental health crisis.

This book contains graphic descriptions of police calls and life situations. The most graphic content is within chapters with titles that represent the NATO alphabet.

Books of influence require a certain amount of information to help people grow, but not to be sensational in the way of airing other people's laundry. There are many variations of family—people who live together who take care of each other. Families have within them secret keepers who honor confidences based on promises withhold information based on their discretion or become the place the secret remains because they forget something only they had known. The people in my family did the best they could with the personalities and skills they had—as did I.

My sole purpose in this book it to share my story as gathered from my perspective to help others grow and learn about themselves. I recognize and respect that members of my family, former colleagues and friends will have their own versions of events. Their stories are fully accessible to them to share on their terms.

Teresa Collins
www.HouseofHyenas.com

BROOK LYNN
you represent the future of women entrepreneurs
you are my skyline

THIS BOOK IS A HOUSE
A HOUSE FOR HYENAS
ITS COVER THE DOOR
THE CONTENTS ARE A KITCHEN TABLE
WHERE YOU CAN SIT AND STRATEGIZE CHANGE
WELCOME

Contents

Introduction

Front Porch

The sky, the ocean, jeans, moons, berries, whales, melancholy, cops, and the last little house on a dead-end street. Blue. Blue. Blue.

Not everything in the world that's blue is true.

Not everything in the world that is blue is beautiful.

Take the term blue blood (think the power of kings, clergy, and males associated with power—and today, police departments). Hundreds of years ago, the wealthy and powerful looked at the veins in their forearms and wrists then decided their blood was different—meaning better—than that of those who toiled the fields. They failed to recognize that since they spent a lot of time indoors the light played with their delicate skin and created a blue look to the river of blood that ran through them.

This difference was something those in power could use to justify their station in life. The workers with sun-baked, weathered skin, aka peasants, could never mirror the same visual effect.

Maybe it was bullshit. Maybe someone in the kingdom's marketing department came up with the phrase 'blue blood'. Now there was a collective noun to justify keeping the drawbridge up and the moat filled.

Blue found its way to 'true blue'—a design brief that worked to encourage loyalty. From there it was pretty much a hop skip and jump to further corruption because, hey! that person is better than you, therefore more powerful. You're not as pure as them. Not as talented. Not as deserving.

You are not enough.

Centuries later, true blue meant a loyalty to staunch conservatism, rule of law, and collectives that require absolute dedication, especially to a hierarchy of rule within police departments. And that's where some of my story resides.

There are people in all parts of society who look at themselves and think they are better than others, then set out to oppress 'others'. Some of them say they are our friends, even our family. Others are our employers. They are no different than those self-righteous, entitled folk of centuries ago. And no matter how subtle, some of us believe them, and then get stuck in an 'I am not enough' or 'I can't follow my dreams' mentality.

Fuck, we've gotta let go of something: blood is not blue.

Blood is the color of a decent Pinot Noir, and as thick as an Appalachian Mamaw's gravy.

I know this because I've attended a lot of crime scenes.

*****

I'm not saying there aren't beautiful blue examples within law enforcement. Day in and day out there are those in uniform who peace-keep and genuinely assist their fellow humans. I've worked with many of those officers.

But much of the true-blue American way I was exposed to in my career was steeped in unwavering die-hard-ness and extreme, overtly conservative practices. That mentality used a lot of fear-fuckery to keep people in categories set up to serve those in power.

Underneath it all, I discovered that a lot of personal attacks—whether at work or in family life—are fear based. I know about these people and the cliques they created within their institutions and spheres of influence.

Truth and duty compelled me to serve in community policing and in my personal life.

Truth, for me is transparent, and it is ever-present in everything I do. It is voice, service, and the formalization of advocacy. It is the result of resilience and determination that began when I was a three-pound preemie born to a teen mom who was into drugs and alcohol, and whose grandparents took responsibility by bringing me home to their little blue house. Truth is not always neatly packaged. My truth involves straying into dangerous territory as a youth, and becoming a teen parent, and rising from my situation to forging a career where I could set examples for those in crisis and make a difference in policing in front line roles and as a detective.

Duty, in my mind, is taking action to keep others safe. From pulling a child's hand away from a stovetop, then talking to them about the danger, to immediately saying yes to a call that backs up colleagues from another police department. It is also serving the self: it includes believing in goodness and finding time in a crazy schedule for self care, and evaluating that schedule, too.

Service, in an ideal world, would be a clear-running stream of compassion and humility. But ideals are subjective. Put a space after the first letter of 'ideal' and it's a phrase: 'I deal' which, in current culture, translates to the corruption of values, benevolence obsolete, twisted transactional.

Service, to me, is not splitting words or dividing people; it is taking what we have in common and using those to do the job at hand, whether it is flipping burgers or investigating a murder—I've done both.

My skills of self-preservation are off the charts, my radar for bullshit is unparalleled, and my experiences are relatable. I am resilient and determined. I have become unmesswithable, essentially an understander of my own world, therefore the ruler of my own world.

We make a life for ourselves and each other through duty and service. We each pour our energy into duty and service, and we steer our lives with our own truth—the foundation of which is based on what we've been told as children.

I am from a family whose first language is hard work, and second tongue is 'let's not talk about our feelings'. Secrets were the norm—there was no realization that holding back vital information just caused more drama and dysfunction, and a whole lot of pain.

Like many families then and now, we were a family of barriers. We essentially stacked emotions and cemented them together with stoicism and fear—we put up walls. Somehow, between all who struggle, suffer, go through patches of bad times that then proliferate into longer stretches, there are so many of these emotional barriers and fear-structures all over the world in so many forms that they might often, to some people, seem to have joined up to be one continuous barrier that blocks the sun from shining on relationships and prevents full-on joy.

I'm gonna take a sledgehammer to that brick wall.

How to Use This Book

The format of this book reflects the formula:

STORY + RESILIENCE + DETERMINATION
= UNMESSWITHABLE.

There are three parts bookended by an introduction (you're in it now) and a conclusion called YOUR HOUSE. Each part is a portion of my life, and includes narratives from a hyena and, later, scripted conversations between me and my higher self. Between each part is an extra section that comprises 'personally experienced police calls' and 'questions received from within a growing sisterhood'.

PART ONE is STORY. My story, in a memoir style, confirms details of my vulnerability. At the end of each biographical chapter in this part are take-aways—things I would not have known at the time, but can see upon reflection.

PART TWO is RESILIENCE, which continues my story, establishes my credibility, and houses advice within the story instead of take-aways. It contains more of the actionable steps, through exampling the qualities that strengthen resilience, and follows the path I took after I received emancipation, then entered legal adulthood.

PART THREE is DETERMINATION, which completes my story by focusing on the strength that comes from STORY + RESILIENCE, reflecting the power for the decision-making process and supercharging the route for future planning.

Following each PART is an EXTRA section containing police calls, questions, and a value commentary/definition all of which are intentionally placed for the continuous overview of my whole purpose. They are well marked if a reader wishes to read them separately.

Threshold

I was born with a force inside me that refuses to settle for average. I am grateful for whatever that force is, without having to understand it. I've come to understand that honoring this force, which is essentially my truth, is not cocky; it is a product of my awareness. I would love for every woman to feel this way about themself.

> Honoring the force in you is not cocky
> it is a product of your awareness.

I've described my story of weakness and strength, and fear and courage, so that people can recognize resilience and determination in themselves. My intention is that readers find strength through what I have experienced and learned. There is value in each of us contributing to a growing sistership where support is second nature, and no one throws anyone under the bus.

True strength of character is built from determination and resilience, which is further fueled by strategy and intuition. This makes our story.

In contributing to a sistership, my mission is:

1. To serve as a leader by encouraging new ideas and forward thinking.

2. To offer support in groups and one-on-one as a certified life coach.
3. To collaborate ideas and troubleshoot with women who are ready to harness their strength.

*****

I'm from a lake-rich, forest-dense State which is a natural home for bears and wolves. So why The House of Hyenas? There are no hyenas in the wild in the USA.

The House of Hyenas because I discovered the freakishly brilliant way hyenas live. Strangely enough, more than two decades ago, I briefly mentioned them at the time of my daughter's birth. I hadn't realized that I'd referenced hyenas until years later, when I was going over some journals.

Once I started studying hyenas, I realized their success was expressible through a formula.

STORY + RESILIENCE + DETERMINATION
= UNMESSWITHABLE

Unmesswithable means never having to be a victim to manipulation. It is being forthright and compassionate with yourself and others. It denotes having high standards and saying 'yes' to discovering your passions. It's about knowing who you are and unapologetically owning it—undeterred by opposition. When you are your true self, you will understand your world, and when you understand your world, you WILL rule it. You will be unmesswithable.

When I applied that to my own life, the results were:

MY STORY + RESILIENCE + DETERMINATION
= AN UNMESSWITHABLE ME

You can apply it to your life. I can help you. The results can be:

YOUR STORY + RESILIENCE + DETERMINATION = AN UNMESSWITHABLE YOU

This book informs and inspires through an unusual format—a combination of memoir *and* self-growth with a generous sprinkling of advocacy, and a side of creativity that includes meeting your higher self. I say memoir and self-growth, but sometimes wonder if I should have said a memoir *of* self-growth.

I am an expert on me, and I want you to be an expert on you. The growth I've been part of, and since mentored, is deeply meaningful to me as the path for others to become stronger.

My wish is for every reader to embrace becoming unmesswithable—whether a reader gets that from comparing their past with the stories of mine, finding gems in those stories, or listening to the hyenas, it matters not. As long as each reader can acknowledge the roles of the naysayers and saboteurs in their lives, and set boundaries, it does not matter.

What counts is that readers begin their journey where they are at and head in the direction of that place where women have made peace with their pasts, fully live their present, and are energized and enthused for their future.

A Hyena Named Story

I, too, was born with a force inside that refused to settle for average. It is the same force that generations of my species, from the savannas of Africa, were born with. My life is spent honoring this force. The force is not egocentric, it is a product of my natural awareness. Every female hyena holds this characteristic.

Misunderstood, undervalued, even condemned by some, we hyenas are one of the most fascinating creatures on the planet because alpha females rule their communities. The girls are the leaders. Not only that, but the cubs spend a long time developing in-utero. That long gestation ensures cubs are wired to thrive from day one. Their big brains memorize the identity and rank of their clan, and each recalls the voice of every member. Organized as a sisterhood, which becomes useful in banding together to protect ourselves, our inherent toughness is balanced with intelligence. This makes it so that we know how to keep the peace and collaborate.

We have a unique feature as a gender—we have evolved male-looking genitals. The organ still functions as a female one—including a birth canal. Simply put, over time, females who had larger, more male-looking genitals survived longer than those without. Natural selection then supported that feature. Some say that this has allowed us to rise and lead because of the visual—appearing as a male.

Others say that the organ gave females a huge advantage in the fierce social system of each hyena species.

Our hyena matriarchal society works because we don't eliminate the males, we simply ELEVATE ourselves. We elevate all of us as a group, as a sisterhood. We support and coach each other, guiding those in our community to a place where they thrive.

For tens of thousands of years, we hyenas have become the most resilient community of animals on earth. We know how to thrive. We are unmesswithable. You cannot break our hearts.

All our cubs are born knowing they are brilliant hyenas. The story they know is of the strength and success of our species. They understand their responsibilities. They never turn on each other.

They never tell themselves stories based on flawed information. They recognize their strengths and, rather than compete against each other, they understand there's enough strength to go around for everyone. Strength isn't a prize that a few hyenas 'win', it is a natural quality that all hyenas discover within themselves.

We hyenas have evolved to see the unmesswithable quality as a powerful beauty in which we rule our own world.

OUR STORY + RESILIENCE + DETERMINATION
= UNMESSWITHABLE US
WE ARE AN UNMESSWITHABLE SISTERSHIP
WITHIN OUR SPECIES

Part One: Story

Living Room

The little blue house I lived in as a child was in an interesting location; it was like the roadbuilders got to the top of a hill and just stopped excavating, prepping, and paving. Pavement, then forest. A road sparsely lined with modest houses, then giant oaks dwarfing Little Blue at its dead end.

Oaks for sure, but it was no 'Hundred Acre Woods'. Nothing about the scene or my life resembled the idyllic world of Christopher Robin and Winnie the Pooh. The Detroit Lakes area was a long way from Pooh Corner—there were real bears… and wolves.

Before my time, when Detroit Lakes, Minnesota was called Detroit—not to be confused with the Motor City in Michigan—wolves and bears would wander the main street of the town. As the town grew the wild creatures retreated to the surrounding forests.

But there were scarier things in my childhood than bears and wolves. There were people I didn't understand, concepts that confused me—hell, I didn't even know they were concepts. There was a general dysfunctional, disconnected, disturbing dynamic around the comings and goings of the people at our house.

There were also pleasant things. Little Blue: the house at the top of the hill, at the end of the dead-end road, had a pretty lawn that was always mowed with precision; potted flowers hung from Little Blue's eaves; rose bushes layered themselves in pinks and reds beneath her windows.

Little Blue looked over her kingdom with a certain pride reserved for tiny houses lived in by folks who worked hard to do their best. Little Blue's position allowed her to hear the happy squeals of children from the two close-by schools—an elementary and a middle school. During the day, for just under an hour at lunch, and two recesses, swings would screech their metal song of movement, and a swooping kind of laughter would come from the slides—happiness in motion. The merry-go round would produce its own child-music of 'go faster' and an extended 'noooooooo' from those wanting off.

When I was a child, I'd sit in a rocking chair that faced a huge pane of glass that windowed the world from our living room—it was a peaceful place to be, and it often seemed the chair rocked itself. There'd be a before-school show: teenagers reaching the top of the hill and the dead-end, a pubescent gaggle of messily dressed boys heading toward the fence that had been cut to allow passage to the school. They'd linger by our oak tree, stop, then drop their backpacks—some boys drinking Coke, others cautiously pulling out Marlborough Reds. Smokes and Cokes before their day in middle school. There was no rush for them, until there sorta was, then they'd toss their half-smoked butts on the ground, swing their packs back over their shoulders, and continue to school.

I'd be looking out at them in the world beyond the living room window, and I'd sit on the rocking chair, eating my generic fruit-loops and dream of that branded boxed cereal that other families had.

The cereal wasn't the only lie; I just didn't know that for sure then. There were seven of us. Six whom I called siblings, and me, the youngest. Nine with the parents. When I was younger, not every member of the family lived in Little Blue, but the house sometimes had a Grand Central Station feel from the dropping in and out.

As the youngest, and a girl, I was encouraged to focus on the pink things in life; to aspire to baking cupcakes and play with dolls.

It angers and fascinates me that this message is still perpetuated in our culture. Back then, the stereotype pushed me into believing I could never have it all. Now that I'm unmesswithable, I know that 'all' has as many meanings as there are people.

TAKE AWAYS
ONE

Our humble beginnings are the X on the map—the place that treasure is buried, the place where our story picks up from those who went before us. It does not have to be painful to go back if we remind ourselves of A.A. Milne's quote in which he has Christopher Robin speaking to Winnie the Pooh.
"Promise me you'll always remember: You're braver than you believe, and stronger than you seem, and smarter than you think."
Christopher Robin said these words to his favorite Bear.

TWO

Few things are more relaxing than sitting on a rocking chair— it can keep time with your heart—and looking out toward your future.

The Bakery

Carol and Gary were born in the early 1940s, and their backgrounds were strongly influenced by a post Second World War life lived by farmers and self-employed bakers who worked night and day to run their homesteads or their bakery.

They met in 1961, married in 1965, and embraced a hard work (at any hour) way of life. Since their parents and grandparents had not exampled intimate family communication, Carol and Gary didn't either. Instead, they remained tied to a way of life that was kind of naïve.

When Carol and Gary had gone out into the world, it was still under the family umbrella. Gary's parents owned the bakery in which Gary worked. Carol began to work there too; there wasn't much opportunity to see beyond the brick and mortar of the building, let alone down the street and outside the small town. At one point in time the bakery burned to the ground and was rebuilt—a testament to their dedication to the family business. Gary's mother worked in that bakery until she was well into her senior years. I truly believe that this generational isolation within their business contributed to the family's lack of knowledge when it came to sharing and positive mental health practices.

As the 60s and 70s brought new attitudes and technology to the world, the bakery was still baking bread. Make no mistake, the world needs freshly baked bread and depends on it, but that kind of work to prepare it requires a sleep-during-the-day, work-all-night schedule, seven days a week. It leaves little time for exploration of the world, and even less to catch the innovations in technology and in psychology. Many people missed out on the sixties' and seventies' wave of 'sharing feelings' because they were completely immersed in running a business 24/7. That part of life passed them by.

They understood hard work, spoke plain language, went to church, followed the old rules. Nothing in their behavior had been adjusted for modern times. Carol and Gary came from solid backgrounds with good people, but those people hadn't learned to communicate about the challenges in life, nor how to share their feelings when emotional issues arose.

When Carol and Gary had their family, they drew from that insulated background. Their children of the 60s and 70s were not completely prepared to meet the rest of the world which had let go of some of the old ways and replaced them with a sense of post-sixties freedom that had traveled from cities like New York and arrived to greet the inexperienced folks of rural Minnesota and the Dakotas.

What I was told about their past is that Carol, married to Gary since 1965, came into the relationship with a son. Gary adopted him, and this child was then considered their first child. Despite any of the dysfunction that arose, Carol and Gary loved each other deeply and dearly, and Gary was dedicated to the boy, Tim.

Carol and Gary were bonded, and cared for each other—clung to each other—and sacrificed for each other. I know that to be true. The other truth is that no one would ever question the work ethic with which they operated.

When the bakery closed, Gary was a policeman for a time, then later returned to the baking business—though not 'his own' bakery. Perhaps this was a return to the familiar, a secure connection to what he had been used to his whole life. He worked nights for many years as a baker in the backrooms of a grocery store; Carol trained to be a nursing assistant—while she had children—and was certified and worked for over three decades in that field.

Between 1965, when they were married, and 1972, they had five children, Tim who had been born to Carol previously, made for six—a family of eight.

TAKE AWAYS
ONE

Be open to all ideas.
Technology and attitudes may be changing fast,
and certain old values will remain golden standards,
but new concepts should always be welcomed and evaluated
be it types of therapy, evolution of speech, or ideas around
living situations.

TWO

Be willing to revisit and evaluate your values.

Hyena

The woods are lovely, dark and deep,
But I have promises to keep,
And miles to go before I sleep,
And miles to go before I sleep.
—Robert Frost.

I love me a little Frost. I mean the literary kind. Keep that cold, white stuff away from me, I'm sub-Saharan don't you know. My species has evolved into clever creatures who run a matriarchal society. Study us and see how our sisterhood operates, apply it to your world, and a large number of western problems would disappear as fast as it takes one of us to take down prey.

Little Blue came into my sightline years before Teresa was born. A small house with the capacity to hold a lot, its manicured lawn a testament to its hardworking owners, Carol and Gary.

My role was to observe and wait. And I did just that. Watched and waited.

Hyenas in the wild live in a den called a cave, or chamber. We raise our cubs in those found shelters. Each of us females gestate our young for 110 days which is longer than many animals of our size and type—our cubs have more time to develop in utero. Two females usually live in a den with as many as twenty cubs at different stages.

Our cubs are born with their eyes open and ready to rock and roll. However, the birthing process is a painful and dangerous event for us and each of our newborns. First-time mothers are at risk simply because of the physiology of the narrow birth canal. Our cubs risk suffocation because of the long journey along that birth canal.

We have our issues as a species in terms of infant mortality, but from the moment we arrive we are unmesswithable. No one can break our stride. As soon as we're born, we explore and interact with our siblings, then set about recognizing the rest of our clan. We interact with our world immediately. Before we are one, we are hunting with our clan—other hyenas with whom we clearly understand our relationship. Because of this, we are self-aware (in animal-world terms)—we know ourselves.

I took my role as a hyena guide seriously. When I arrived to wait for Teresa, Carol and Gary were dealing with an awful lot. They had a large family and full-time jobs that involved shiftwork. This did not help them come together often as a whole, Work. Work. Work. Provide. Provide. Provide. There were more mouths than money.

Hyenas in the wild live in the moment. We adjust to the times, or we die. Human life has more wiggle room. Carol and Gary faced challenges with some of their children. The world outside Little Blue held many temptations and dangers for children who were being raised in a life a decade or two behind the times.

When their second child, Shelly, was a teenager, she presented a disruptive personality and began to use drugs. Carol and Gary found it difficult to cope with Shelly's behavior. When she missed a lot of school, and when drugs became a major problem for her, they arranged for her to live in group home and, when she discovered she was pregnant, she went to live at another group home until after the baby was born.

All the humans in Shelly's life received Shelly's version of how her pregnancy came to be. There was a sadness attached to skepticism regarding her stories.

As a hyena guide, I was given the background that I was given. What I knew is there would be a baby. I was to wait for that baby.

While I waited outside Little Blue, expecting a Christmassy arrival, I had to change my plan. I thought I had some time to learn more about my role as her guide, but there was word that she had been born prematurely in Fargo, North Dakota. She wasn't coming home right away.

My Teresa was not with me. I was not with her. Not in the way we were meant to be together. I improvised.

I trekked the thirty miles cross country, half the trip in the woods, skirting the northern edge of Big Cormorant Lake, and avoiding highway 94. The other half was through field after field set aside for spring wheat, canola, and barley. The fall colors were spectacular deep greens, oranges, and golds. Crisp leaves crunched into a soft mattress for me when I slept under a fall sky.

I tried to get in through the main doors, then the exit doors, but I could not penetrate the building. I found a good spot outside the hospital in some bushes at the cornerstone of the foundation. Each morning the autumn wind would whip around and wake me, then threaten snow. I'd shake off the frosty coating then head to the entrance, pacing and watching. Night after night I curled up tighter than the one before and sent lullaby messages to My Teresa.

Meanwhile, Shelly returned to Detroit Lakes with Carol and Gary.

A month or so later, when I knew Teresa was going to be released, I retraced my steps home to Little Blue.

Not long after Teresa came home to Little Blue, Shelly began to date someone. She indicated to Carol and Gary that she was going to move away with this person. Gary and Carol said it would not be safe for Teresa. There was an agreement made. A lawyer was hired, and an adoption took place. Carol and Gary, Teresa's grandparents, became her legal parents.

The problem was, Carol and Gary never told Teresa this. To make things even more complicated, they'd often tell Teresa that Shelly was a friend of the family, or infer Shelly was one of their children but had run away to the circus.

That was an odd thing to say about one of their children to their grandchild. Carol and Gary were extremely competent and responsible in many ways, but somehow unable to organize themselves around more modern-day talk about feelings, coping skills, and family dysfunction.

It was not until Teresa was much older that they shared that Shelly was Teresa's biological mother and, even then, it was not done formally but in casual way like, 'oh, by the way, she's your biological mother.' There was no sitting down with Teresa at an early age to say, 'when you were born, your birth-mommy, our daughter, had become addicted to drugs and so we took over the parenting and are your grandparents. Your birth-mother is Shelly, and she is our daughter. She's the young woman that sometimes comes around here.'

Carol and Gary raised Teresa as their own, with Teresa calling them Mom and Dad. Teresa's aunts and uncles were known to her as brothers and sisters. Those aunts and uncles aligned with their parents' story—they'd been kids themselves when Shelly had been pregnant. Shelly went on to have two more daughters.

They didn't keep the information from Teresa because they were trying to be mean or calculating nor did they want to cause harm. They just went about the simple ways they had learned when they were growing up.

When I go way back to Teresa's arrival, I wanted to call her T-rex because I knew how strong she'd been to survive her birth, and how strong she'd have to be, but T-minus came to me as I cursed some of the decisions made in that house. I howl-cried over them. T-minus the truth was more accurate.

There is energy in everything. Little Blue felt the weight of the family dynamics on her floorboards and, over the years, listened to the struggles via slammed doors.

I worried about that young woman who dropped in from time to time and shook the foundation of them all with her issues of addiction. I wondered if she would tell Teresa. I worried about Tim and his feelings of displacement in that he'd arrived with Carol when she married Gary, yet no one was aware of that except for Carol, Gary, and Tim. And even though Gary had adopted Tim, the lack of openness and communication snaked secrets through Little Blue and created power-struggles between the children who lived in her. I worried about them all, but I was there for Teresa.

Poor communication and sharing issues between family members caused a ripple of sadness that even spread out to the trees around me.

They loved her. Yes. They had rescued, saved, stepped in because they'd had to. But she was their cub's cub.

Oh, I howled it. Bayed it to the moon: 'Those who you call Mom and Dad are your grandparents. That young woman is your biological mother.'

There had been family stress from the day-to-day management of work and children. Teresa grew up in a household where several of the children became involved with drugs and alcohol.

I worried it was a matter of time.

Teresa's grandparents were down-to-earth folks who simply didn't know what they didn't know. They went about their work without a sense of discovery—there were no parenting courses or peer support that they considered accessing. They ran the family-show as their own parents had run theirs: work, pay the bills, send the children to school, do not attend the children's activities (because they were working or too tired), make sure the yard and exterior were perfectly presented with a pride of ownership.

Sometimes Little Blue was like Grand Central Station with adult children coming and going. Many times, I'm sure I heard Little Blue sigh as it held all the pain of each of its occupants.

Sometimes, I'd sneak up to the front window at night, when they were all in bed, and I would push my thoughts through that big glass window: you are T-more-than-enough, you are T-love, T-plus, T-future. Then I'd catch the scent of the roses Teresa's grandparents raised with so much care, squish a nose-print on the windowpane, then slip back into the woods.

In Africa, a guide is called a kiongozi. A mentor is mshauri. Like all humans, she was born to learn; I was around to help her reach her full potential—and embrace the role of guide. To merge with me—me who was a part of her. I didn't know when she'd know that I was. Hell, I didn't know when that would be.

In the beginning, I wished I had more power than just observing; I wanted to swirl myself into a storm and pick up the house at the end of the street and tornado it away. Sometimes I wanted to rush through Little Blue's front door and grab Teresa and carry her off to raise as my own. It's good that I wasn't given that power because I now know:

It was never a dead end. It was a beginning.

We were an unlikely couple: my roots in the African savanna, hers in the USA—the Midwest. Perhaps it was intentional that we were combined so that we comprised worldliness from the start. I only know that, when she arrived, it was my responsibility to guide her through her childhood, adolescence, and beyond, until she honed the art of guiding herself, and then became a leader who guided others. It was my job to protect, lead, and teach her so that when she reached a certain time and place—and I didn't know when or where that would be—we would merge then move on to help others in a way neither of us understood back then.

I was there from the start because she was born to become a mshauri ~ mentor... a kiongozi—a guide.

Kitchen

It was the hub. Like all homes in the 70s and 80s and into the 90s, the phone was attached to the wall; most conversations with the outside world originated and terminated there. Its coiled cord stretched all the way to the kitchen table—a table never meant for eating at.

That table was the place where Mom and Dad filed paperwork, piled unread mail, and stacked magazines. It was space for extra storage containers to be stored for current projects Mom had going on—think: both organized and unfinished. Its surface held mail—opened and unopened—lists, flyers, and school notes to be signed. And at that table, more often than not, was Mom in a nightgown, a cigarette in her mouth or between her fingers, the phone cradled to her ear.

The kitchen was the point of entry for good news and bad news to arrive at the house. That's likely where Mom and Dad received the news—over the phone—that their teenager, Shelly, was pregnant.

Shelly would have been fifteen or sixteen when she delivered that news. Dad would have been 38, and Mom 41.

I was born on October 5, 1982, at the main hospital in Fargo, North Dakota. I was so small that I could fit into the palm of an adult's hand. I stayed in the hospital for about a month, The plan was that once I was 'home' Shelly would take me to daycare and then go to work or school. Once I was 'home', Shelly had her own idea and decided she would move in with her new boyfriend. Her parents—my grandparents—the people I would know and call Mom and Dad, told her that she would not be able to take me.

I had no idea of that official adoption until many years later.

Basically, before my first birthday, my grandparents became my legal parents. I'm sure those papers were stacked on that kitchen table too. And Shelly? Well, from toddlerhood onwards, all I knew was that occasionally there was a girl who came to the house who Mom and Dad would call 'Shelly, the girl who ran away to the circus.'

Until I was brought home from the hospital, the youngest child in the house was Jason; he was ten. Who knows what he thought when a baby arrived and stayed—he was certainly displaced as the youngest, yet he would have known his mother hadn't been pregnant, but maybe he didn't know that his sister, Shelly, had been. In his eyes, I must have magically arrived and taken over his role as the youngest in the family.

TAKE AWAYS
ONE

Be aware of the influence of displacement within families,
and recognize the impact change has on
each person's role—encourage conversation around it.

TWO

Figure out the safe spaces in your life;
the parts of your home you feel most comfortable

having difficult conversations in—build in a ritual of safety,
be it a cup of tea, deep breathing, or other preparation for
those conversations
with yourself or others.

Garden Space

Jason is the sibling I have the most memories of during my younger years. I knew him as Jay. In the summer months of Jay's teenage years, he'd cut his t-shirts into tank tops and parade around showing off a fresh buzz cut while flaunting a strong, tall, athletic build. He and his friends were obsessed with wrestling—watching it, imitating the celebrity ones, and fighting with each other.

Boys—some bald, some round, some skinny—came up the hill and gathered in the outdoor space between Little Blue and its garage. It was the perfect place for their wrestling ring—the softest green grass, and flat enough for theatrics.

Some came to fight, some came to watch. The boys would pick their teams and begin the grappling. The best way to describe the shenanigans was a bunch of sweaty teen boys trying to fulfill their dreams and fantasies of becoming professional wrestlers. Grunting, grappling, sweating, swearing, all while tapping each other in and out of the make-believe wrestling ring.

Then, suddenly, the song for Hulk Hogan would come on, the back door would burst open, and out would walk Jay who I'd later discover was really my uncle. He'd take giant steps while waving his hands in the air. His red and yellow hulk T-shirt had become a tank. He'd fill his lungs with air and then his voice would boom: "Whatcha gonna do when Hulkmania runs wild on you?"

All the other boys would cheer loudly, visibly becoming increasingly nervous as he got closer to the ring. It was like watching it on the television.

It was a little terrifying to watch. But then that is exactly what living with Jay was like.

The next thing I knew, Jay became a different person within a short period of time. Not years, but months. Looking back, I think he'd maybe been angry, and then became angrier. For a while I just thought he was being too cool, but as I got more perspective, later in life, I often wonder if he was resentful over my arriving and somehow taking the attention from him.

Little Blue served as more than a wrestling venue, and a perfectly groomed lawn and awesome rose garden—it was my pretend-to-be-a-pop-star studio where I'd watch MTV music videos and then take my little black boombox and mixed tapes outside. The songs on the cassettes were recorded from the radio by me. I'd always try to get a whole song without the DJ making announcements. It was magic for me—all the songs I loved mashed into the little black ribbon that ran through the plastic case. Side one of the tape was the practice side and side two had all the good songs from the most popular artists at that time. TLC and Salt 'n Peppa were my favorites. The play list—I called the dance list—had Hootie And The Blow Fish, The Spice Girls, and Alanis Morissette.

I would set that black boom box up in the front yard that overlooked the other houses down hill from ours. This put me on a kind of raised stage to create the best choreographed moves ever created. Not only did I dance, I belted out the lyrics. I'd sing like I was Left Eye in TLC—I'd even put a patch over my eye. Not a condom wrapper though, as my hero in TLC did. If I'd have ever done that, I knew Dad would have had something to say, and my behind would have been sore.

Before Destiny's Child there was TLC, and they were 'crazy, sexy, cool'. I never knew the reasons TLC fans pinned a condom or condom package on their clothing—I just knew I wanted to—even though I didn't know what condoms were.

Years after their performances, one of the surviving band members said their condom-wearing fashion choices were spur of the moment. Apparently, one day, Lisa 'Left Eye' Lopez came to meet the rest of the band and had a condom pinned on her. From then on, that became their thing. It became a talking point in magazine interviews and MTV sit-downs, which meant that everyone was talking about safe sex.

Usually talking about safe sex sounds like an after-school special (during which kids zone out), but when TLC did it, people listened.

TLC found a creative way to bring awareness to an issue; their actions influenced others. At that time, AIDS was sweeping through the country. TLC understood kids listened to performers. They believed they had duty to provide critical information that could save lives. And that they did so in a way that was eye-catching.

The thing is, I didn't know what sex was, let alone safe sex. I didn't know what condoms were for. I was naïve and didn't want to look silly by asking. I just went along with what everyone talked about. I didn't know how babies were made. I was the girl behind the glass looking out to the lawn, or the girl on the lawn dancing and singing. I settled with a makeshift patch. I created routines, then danced my heart out. I'd dance all afternoon and keep going—the streetlights simply changed the ambiance for a 'night show'.

When I wasn't dancing I was on roller skates playing drive-in restaurant. I'd gather plastic plates and cups from the house. The old Tupperware containers used for those bagged, generic fruit loops were my favorite containers. I would then grab a pitcher of water and go outside. The driveway was long and, at that time, recently paved with concrete and a fresh coat of black sealant. I would skate around the drive, taking orders from all my 'customers' and delivering them cups of water served from an old plastic Christmas tray.

Jay would do his thing, I would do mine, but then the oddest thing would happen. I would be dancing or serving my customers in the driveway, and he would ambush me. He'd throw me down to the ground and put wrestling moves on me until I screamed and cried. It happened often. I didn't think too much of it other than this is what brothers do to their little sisters. But I began to fear him, watching for where he was and figuring out how to avoid him.

Jay continued to change. He went out a lot. I don't know why he was gone so much, and I don't know where he went or what he did; it just came to be that he was rarely seen. When he was home, his anger grew. I likened him and his anger to a pot of potatoes on the boil—it would simmer then, gradually, the white starchy water would boil over, spewing out the lid and boiling over onto the stove, causing the burner to hiss and flame. Though Jay's moods and behavior affected me, along with the way each of the individual members of my family had shaped me, I began to understand a little more about how we ticked—yet I was still confused about the family dynamics.

TAKE AWAYS
ONE

If there's something deep inside that is messengering you that
something from the past doesn't feel right,
give yourself permission to investigate it. You can choose to let
it go
or take action once you have shed light on it for yourself.

TWO

Never underestimate the power of play.
Take yourself for ice cream, play at a playground,
build a pillow fort in your living room and take a nap in it.

Craft Room

Sure, it was the kitchen, but it was so much more when the aunt I knew as my sister, Tonia, took the time to do an important project with me.

Tonia had long, reddish-brown hair which was always styled for the times: big. Aquanet hairspray—a standard in the basement bathroom—was responsible for the hair-do's consistency.

Tonia was active, a dancing queen in legwarmers and white shoes. She listened to music from the 80s: Bon Jovi, Poison, and Aerosmith. I loved watching her kick her legs in the air as if she was a member of a dance line. Maybe this is where my love of dancing came from—it makes sense because she appeared so free, talented, and happy. She resembled a rockstar with all that hair spray and the legwarmers.

Tonia was a nurturer; kind and caring. One of my fondest memories was when she helped me with an elementary school project for Valentine's Day. I had been given specific words to incorporate into the project. When I told Tonia about it, I explained that I didn't want to do the typical shoe-box-wrapped-with-paper that everyone did each year—the kind that had a hole cut in the top so that other kids could 'mail' their valentines to each other. I wanted something different, something creative, something no one else had done.

Tonia found an empty cookie tin—the kind people put buttons or other bits and pieces into—then she found some tag-board (poster board—the thick, large paper that can take permanent marker and stand up to having things glued to it). I don't know why we always seemed to have tag board around the house, but we did.

She cleared a space on the table we never ate at, and she piled all kinds of supplies on it so that we could create a Valentine's masterpiece. We talked about different ideas but none of them seemed extravagant enough. Then, Tonia took on an inspired look and began by drawing a large heart on white poster board. It was a perfect heart, not lopsided or off balance. It was Tonia perfect, and I loved it. I remember so clearly, even though its decades ago: Tonia read the wordlist and then said, "Yes, this will do."

She handed me the scissors. I cut out the white heart—all the while being extra cautious not to be sloppy with my cutting; I was determined to keep the heart as perfect as when she had drawn it. When I'd cut the whole thing out it more than covered my entire face. Meanwhile, she was writing and talking, creating a poem, making sure to use the words I'd been given. After a few re-writes she had the most beautiful poem that met the assignment's requirements. She wrote it in pencil onto the heart I'd cut out.

Her beautiful writing looked like that of a young woman's letter to a lover. The lines were perfect, her letters were a mix of bubbly and cursive, connecting in just the right spots. Tonia's pressure on the paper, the size and slope of her letters were magnificent, and any letters that were the same mirrored each other perfectly.

I, ever-so-carefully, delicately traced over her handwriting with a red permanent marker. When I'd finished the red, I took a black marker and underlined each of the assigned words just to make sure the teacher would clearly see them and know that I understood the assignment.

Once the writing and tracing was complete, I caught the scent of something burning—not smoky but more chemical. Over on the kitchen counter, the counter cluttered with the Tupperware containers, Tonia had a few clear cylinders each a bit smaller than a cigarette. She would take each one and push it into the end of a weird device that was plugged into the wall. Next, she held the device and showed me how it resembled a gun. She helped me depress the trigger which caused the solid cylinder to move along a section of the gun and melt out of the nose or barrel in a clean line of glue. I'd never known there was such thing as a glue gun.

We outlined the entire heart with the glue and placed a ribbon of white lace around the outer edges. Then we incorporated the container to catch the Valentine's mail.

The heart was perfect, the writing was perfect, the poem was perfect. Its simplicity made it so. But it wasn't the tag board, the lace, the writing, or the glue gun that made this so memorable. It was Tonia. Tonia made this what it was. She took the time. She cared. She loved me before, during, and after the project. She never made an excuse not to help me. She listened to my ideas of what I wanted, and she helped me make it come true.

More than three decades ago and I still clearly remember the close-together feeling—and cherish it.

There are golden moments and sparkling normals in life. Sometimes we think we have to search for them between all the cluttered counters and messy paraphernalia on a kitchen table, then go into the tiniest places where gratitude and love are huddled close as if hiding between great voids of dysfunction. But they are not really hiding. They are tucked away in those spots because we are afraid they will be taken away from us—even though they have attached themselves to our hearts forever.

Tonia moved out and married. She had a daughter. Those mornings at the big picture window in the living room—the same one from which I watched the cool kids hunkering down around the big oak tree (while I ate my generic fruit loops)—I would watch Tonia carry her daughter, Terrenna, on her hip, a bag on her other shoulder, all the way up our driveway. Every workday between seven and seven-thirty.

Mom was rarely awake at this time, Dad not home from his night shift at the bakery. Terrenna would hang around with me, and then I'd head to school. When I'd come home from school, Terrenna would still be there, but Mom would have left for work; Dad would be getting some rest before his nightshift. The care fell to whomever was around, and that included me.

Every evening of every weekday, Tonia would pick up her daughter.

I always wondered why Mom and Dad would take this on, but I only asked myself—never anyone else. I kept thinking, they've raised their children, they work extremely hard, yet they have agreed to be responsible for a toddler. I told myself maybe this is what parents do for their children.

At that time, I didn't know that's what they were doing with me—even more than that. They had me fulltime.

Occasionally, I'd go to where Tonia lived with her husband. They had a trailer just outside of town. Seeing as it was a trailer, it was long; I always felt like the walls were closing in on me. Its narrow hallways led to tiny rooms. It made Little Blue look huge.

Most of the time the trailer-house was in shambles. Boxes crammed into the hallways leaving even less space for walking. More boxes were piled to the ceiling in other rooms. But it was their home. And home is where the heart is. And Tonia's heart was there. And judge-ey as I may have been, I could put up with an infinite number of messy rooms as repayment for the experience of the Valentine's Day project of years before.

Once Tonia was married and was a parent, her priorities had to change. She was a grown up. Long gone were the legwarmers and dancing sessions. When I'd go to the trailer it was to babysit while Tonia and her husband went out for an evening. I was told not to go outside the house to play with the other kids—this might have had to do with the neighborhood.

Tonia's trailer was the nicest in the trailer park—that was something. When I was younger, it seemed she lived there a long time but, looking back, she didn't—funny how time in childhood passes so differently than when we're adults. Shortly after she moved there, she left her husband and took her daughter with her. She'd met someone else.

Tonia and her new partner moved to another town, but it was close enough that I did see her quite often. Again, it was to babysit and to be a house cleaner. Tonia had two more children with her partner.

And then there came to be a crisis. My beautiful Tonia was nowhere to be found. Her husband had not seen her and one of her children in weeks—she left their two with him. She hadn't called anyone. She hadn't been to work. She and her daughter, Terrenna, had disappeared into thin air. Weeks turned to months. Mom and Dad searched for her. They hired a private detective.

Tonia's disappearance took its toll on Mom and Dad. When they weren't driving around looking for her, they were on the phone trying to find her. The police were at our house frequently to speak with them.

Months went by. The investigator still could not locate Tonia.

I would often find Mom crying at the kitchen table late at night. She would sift through Tonia's papers and belongings that Tonia's husband had provided. She'd look at them over and over to see if she could find clues of where Tonia might be. Meanwhile, Dad—the strong, unemotional man—tried to comfort Mom. They always remained optimistic that they would find her, but the stress, fear, and worrying tested their marriage significantly.

One evening, when Dad was in his recliner eating his TV dinner and watching the news, and Mom was at the kitchen table smoking her cigarette and drinking a cup of coffee, I noticed a car coming toward the house. I was sitting in the rocking chair in front of that big picture window that looked out onto the world. There was a knock at the door and a man in a suit entered. Mom and Dad sat with the man at the cluttered kitchen table where we never ate, and I was told to go to my room. My room was located just off the kitchen, so I was in earshot of what was being said even with the door closed.

Low voices in a few moments of conversation led to Mom bursting out crying. Dad continued to ask questions to the man in the suit. There was paper shuffling—and I must have opened the door a crack because I know that the man had produced those papers from envelopes. He began to review them with Mom and Dad. The man's tone was not a 'she's dead' sound but contained some positivity. There was some relief in their breaths. Based on that, I felt I could slowly exit my bedroom and test the water. I walked back into the living room and sat in the rocking chair in front of the picture window. I pretended to watch television—which was still on. The investigator told Mom and Dad that even though he had been able to pick up Tonia's trail he hadn't been able to locate her. But he knew she was alive. She had remained one step ahead of him. Though I gathered that she was with another man, and they were hiding from something, I have never known the details. All these years later, I have no idea why Tonia was 'on the run—Terrenna in tow, with another guy.

Despite all this, Tonia and the memory of the Valentine's Day project lives in my heart. Many decisions in my life were made because of Tonia's kindness. Her actions were part of the foundation of my compassion.

TAKE AWAYS
ONE

Give your time to someone—young or old—in a project.
Your dedication will net you as much pleasure as they receive.
It can be something as simple as helping someone write thank you notes,
completing a photograph album, or making cookies.

TWO

Tell people how much they mean to you.
Single out a time in your history when you were moved by something they did.
This could be a teacher
family member, neighbor, a leader, or coach.
If you recall a time that impacted you,
no matter how small, the sharing will brighten your life and theirs
(if the person is no longer living you can share your gratitude
with their family).

Hyena

I shall be telling this with a sigh
Somewhere ages and ages hence:
Two roads diverged in a wood, and I—
I took the one less traveled by,
And that has made all the difference.
– Robert Frost
Excerpt from *The Road Not Taken*

Frost said everything he'd learned about life could be said as 'life: it goes on.' One of the most powerful things that he said that reflects our evolving into a strong species is:

"The best way out is always through."

I watched Teresa watch her 'Mom' cry at the kitchen table. I thought about Frost's talking about the going 'through'. Teresa was going through life, and I was determined she would get through it all to come out the other side and succeed, then use her experiences. Of course, she didn't know that I was doing that—no one really knows they have a guardian angel or guide or the energy of love around them in the way that other-worldly stuff works, because they're too busy getting through.

There were times when Tonia had spent time with Teresa that the whole world breathed softer breaths because a child, Teresa, felt safe. At those times I could curl up and sleep for a while knowing that Tonia was nurturing Teresa and connecting with her. Teresa needed it. That Valentine's Day project was such a beautiful sight to witness. Tonia was completely dedicated to making Teresa's dream come true. And, by the way, there are no little dreams. Having a special project to take into school was massive for Teresa, and it turned out that the connection and love shared that day was bigger than Valentine's Day. Teresa felt proud of herself, so careful was she with the tracing and cutting, and Tonia was proud of herself too. They were helping each other in a house that didn't experience a lot of emotional connection. The warmth generated by their working together melted a little of the February snow around Little Blue—I know because I lapped a little up to experience part of that elixir of family love.

But when Tonia was missing, I could feel Teresa's fear. My role, job, assignment, road—whatever anyone wants to call it—was to stay with Teresa. But I knew the woods and the surrounding area from when I'd tracked through Minnesota when Teresa was born and had to stay in the hospital.

My heart ached for Carol and Gary too. They were doing the best they could, and their world was upside down, again, with a missing daughter.

That night, when Teresa was in the rocking chair, and that car came down the driveway, I trailed the man who came up to the house, but I could not get a sense of whether Tonia was okay or not. So, I watched through the window, again, and became hypnotized by Teresa in the rocking chair—back and forth, back and forth, rocking through her fear.

And she did. Teresa's resilience kicked in. Deep inside, she didn't know that she knew that resilience was about more than survival, and that her ability to move through this family emergency was based on experiences she'd had that had strengthened her. Of course, some of those experiences were the times of positivity spent with Tonia—yes, the Valentine's Day project which had anchored Teresa in connection. I was ever grateful to Tonia for that. It had planted seeds for strength that would help Teresa deal with whatever was to follow.

The hardest part for a guide or guardian angel type of observer-protector is that it's seemingly impossible to break the rules. I wanted to rush in, break through the door and curl up beside My Teresa, but that's not how it works. She had to find me without me just jumping out and saying, 'Don't be scared, I'm not going to hurt you, don't freak out even though I'm a wild animal standing next to you when you're outside, and by your window when you're inside.'

She had to find me in her own time, on her own terms.

So, I spoke to the siding on the house, and to the trees, and the beautiful roses in the summer, and to the mice under the earth under the snow in the winter, and I hoped she'd hear me telling her how amazing she was. How strong she was. Her resilience was over the top, but she was shutting down from not having her feelings validated.

An amazingly constructed tent that survives basecamps on Mt. Everest is resilient, as are the shelters erected to withstand the conditions of the savanna where my species is from.

Hyenas and humans are not tents, and neither are guides and guardian angels (if you believe in them). Hyenas and humans are sentient beings—they feel things. Teresa had daily lessons: Adversity 101 and then went on to Advanced Adversity. The house was a roof over her head but there was no one under who could do connected-attention, validation, cheer-the-child-on, or soothe a child's fears.

The House at the Lake

As a pre-teen, I'd climb into Dad's truck, and he'd drive to Tammy's house for the weekend. I loved going there; the drive seemed long, and we'd listen to Johnny Cash while my father chain-smoked Marlboro Lights. The windows were always rolled up and I'd choke my way there. There'd never be any conversation, just Cash and Cigarettes, and what felt like days driving down a highway that was surrounded by tall trees, lakes, and ponds.

No conversation still meant I'd ask at least a dozen times during the drive, "How much longer?"

I always knew we were close when I spotted the giant fish at the side of the road. This fish was the size of a trailer pulled by a semi—maybe it was a trailer from a semi. It was painted to look like a walleye. The mouth of the fish was wide open and there was a door in the mouth. I always wondered what was inside that door. Was it a restaurant, a bar, was it hollow on the inside? To this day I still do not know the answer to this. But that fish is still there. Now there's something for my bucket list.

Tammy lived in the middle of a forest whose driveway led to a child's paradise. There were campers and cabins everywhere. Each spot was a neat plot with green grass and fine sand. There were open fields with flowers. At night fireflies lit up the fields like millions of little stars had fallen to earth to flicker in a private show for me.

There were volleyball courts beyond a playground with swings and teeter- totters. Kids my age—eleven-ish—were driving golden golf carts, eating popsicles, and running around in their bathing suits. The massive paradise featured a large swimming pool with children and teenagers chasing each other around the cool, blue water, holding their noses as they jumped in.

Next to the pool was a large, red, three-storey building. As men and women went in and out of the main door it banged like thunder. Some of the people were carrying fishing poles, others had children on their hips, while many of the people had a beer in their hands.

Beyond those doors was a large staircase that went up to the second floor where there was music playing through decent speakers. Pool tables were scattered around, and cocktail tables with chairs took up space beyond a bar. Teens played pool and darts, and they slipped quarters into a jukebox. The smell of pizza filled the air. Laughter made the music hard to hear.

Past the pool table the windows offered a view of a huge lake that looked like an ocean. The sun's beams bounced off the lake, the boats, the people, and the windows themselves—everything and everyone was sun-kissed. Boats would come in and out of the bay then dockhands would appear and get started on cleaning fish for the fishermen.

When I was hungry, I'd run up to the hidden doors behind the bar and pick out a frozen pizza, hand it to the lady or man working behind the bar, then play pool while the pizza cooked.

After eating, I would disappear back into the forest or head down to the docks. I was able to swim all day in the hot summer sun, ride a bike through the forest on all the 4-wheeler trails, drive golf carts through the trails, often stopping to say hello to everyone. Every time I visited Tammy's I'd look for friends I'd previously made.

In the evenings, Tammy and her husband would all gather in the house for dinner and conversation. A lot of the conversation focused on hunting and fishing spots.

I loved watching Tammy. I loved watching her cook and clean up. She made meals Mom and Dad never attempted to make.

I loved seeing the caring way she and her husband interacted with each other.

I loved the way her home was so put together.

I looked up to Tammy. She appeared to be living an amazing, loving lifestyle. I wanted to be her when I grew up. As I aged, Tammy and I didn't see each other as often, but later in life we rekindled our relationship and formed a meaningful friendship as women.

TAKE AWAYS
ONE

The things we used to love to do are great signs for what we might like to do tomorrow.

TWO

We need sisters. They don't have to be biological.
Sisterhood helps us help each other form bonds and, through that,
we can positively change the world.
We need to find our sisters and create sisterhood groups
so that when there is a cry for help, for kindness,
for justice, we can seamlessly come together as one tribe.

Visitation Room

The earliest memory I have of Darcie is going to visit her while she was in a treatment center. I remember going into a concrete building with Mom and Dad, then walking through a damp hallway into a dimly lit room. We passed a lot of people who were sitting at tables and speaking in little groups—groups of females. I assumed young girls were being visited by their family members, but I don't remember asking about it later, nor do I recall Mom or Dad sharing or enlightening me.

I walked up to her as she sat at the table, then leaned in and gave her a hug. Mom and Dad did the talking; I have no idea about what—we weren't there long.

They never talked about why she was there.

The way things were dealt with was simply to go through the hard times, sweep them under a rug, and assume everyone would one day forget about it.

There is no forgetting. Stuff piles up for everyone. For the Tims, the Shellys, the Tonias, Tammys, Darcies, Jasons, and Teresas.

What I choose to remember about Darcie is that she had a way of making the best out of her situations. She enjoyed the outdoors, and worked hard, and made things fun.

When I was still a child, Darcie had a son. It was kind of unique to think that I was an auntie to 'my' nephew—at that time it's how I saw it because I believed Darcie was my sister.

While official titles of what we are to each other are not the most important thing, the clarity of biological relationships is important when we're working on our own identity—and we're especially working on our identity when we're children.

What I do remember is that, early on, Darcie lived in a house that was just a couple blocks away from Little Blue. I could walk there if I walked the roadway home from school instead of cutting through the fence line.

I was still a child when Darcie had her second son. Unfortunately, Darcie had a difficult time maintaining relationships. There was a lot of fighting between Darcie and her husband.

A divorce ensued. I was confused because I was often in the middle of things. I would babysit the boys right before their father would come to get them for the exchange so they could spend time with their dad.

I recall that even though she played the tough person, the breakup upset her. She would cry. She would be so upset. And she'd yell and argue too. It scared me.

Our stories involve what we have witnessed, and through a lens that is tinted by the influence of our family of origin. I can only respond to what I saw and then correlate it to how it played a role in my life—even how the relationships I witnessed in my childhood played a role into my teenage and adult decisions.

Darcie later married another man, and she had a third boy. Our whole family loved this man. He was into NASCAR racing and didn't seem to do a whole lot of outdoor activities as Darcie had done, but they would go out together and I would babysit.

I liked going to her house during this time. She always had the good food, the kind I didn't often get at home. The good bread with the soft crust; the good hotdogs; brand-name soda. It was great because I could walk in the back door and into the kitchen and the fridge was right there. That was always my first stop for an ice-cold Pepsi. I remember Darcie drinking a lot of Pepsi too.

Over the years, this relationship too dissolved and turned nasty. I remember the same turmoil I witnessed with her other relationships. The house was a mess of boxes, swearing, and chaos. I got the impression that it was harder or more painful than her other breakups, but, of course, being one of the family who never talks about things, she never talked about it. Instead, she yelled, argued, and fought.

Darcie had a number of relationships that she thought would work; even had more children and long-term relationships that seemed like they'd be forever ones.

Darcie continued to visit us at Little Blue. It seemed she was happy, always talking about the good things in life. Eventually it seemed to me that she was in a long-term relationship. I remember saying to myself that, when I was older, that's the kind I wanted: a hard-working partner with a successful career, and no financial pressure.

But not long after everything seemed great, Darcie came for a visit. She complained to 'Dad' about her husband's work. She said she needed to change her lifestyle. I wasn't that old, but I recall getting a little upset and frustrated listening to her complain about this. I went off on her. I began to yell at her, and we bantered back and forth, and some names were called, but what I remember the most was telling her—and cockily—that she might have to stop using brand-name shampoo and conditioner and use the Walmart stuff. We got face to face arguing until my dad jumped in to split it up. I was so enraged because she had this wonderful man that took in her boys and dated her while she was pregnant, was there for her during the birth of her daughter, then had another child with her. I was flabbergasted she was being so negative about a situation. It seemed to be all about how it was going to affect her living, rather than being grateful for her spouse, her children, and the great life she was living.

I had not expressed my anger like that before. It was unusual for me. Scary, too. But it stands out in my memory.

I wish I'd known that Darcie's life was hers to live. It played out based on her own experiences in early life and the genetics that created her as well.

It came to be that Darcie had five boys and one girl. Sadly, one of the boys—a twin—was stillborn. She raised them with as positive an attitude as she could, given her circumstances. Darcie showed up for her children. No matter how difficult her relationships were, she was an excellent mom, doing everything with her kids—lots of activities. Those children were given so many opportunities and I love that about her.

TAKE AWAYS
ONE

Lessons are repeated until they are learned.
Cycles continue until they are broken.

TWO

Our stories and our judgements of others, and our anger,
is all part of who we are.

Hyena

"Most of the change we think we see in life
is due to truths being in and out of favor."
–Robert Frost

Out at the Golden place, after Teresa finished dinner with Tammy and family, she'd take a jar into the big open field. She'd burst into a sprint across it, and sweep at her leg with her hand, thinking the feeling was lengths of grass smoothing against her calves, but it was me running so close to her, and in a rhythm, that my short hair would be touching her leg, and then she'd be skimming her hand across my back, not realizing that's what it was. Honestly, sometimes I had to be careful not to trip her.

Those were such beautiful times when, for a moment (and then another), I'd think she'd see me, or wonder if she'd stop to look right beside her, but she was running... chasing the fireflies, wanting to capture them in her jar—and she was busy questioning.

When she did stop and question how these little flying things could light up at night, I sat at her heels, enchanted by how she lit up the world. She was My Teresa.

I loved how she forgot all about her sadnesses when she was at the Golden place. She just wanted to live in paradise by the lake. So did

I. When she was at the Golden place, she pretended she lived there. So did I… I mean, that we both lived there… together.

Golden's opposite, in the form of the color gray, surfaced on her visits with Darcie, in a dull place surrounded by mystery. No one told Teresa anything. She'd go into that building and I would not know how to get into it to be beside her. I'd pace, I'd stand on my hind legs to stretch and look inside the building, but the windows—what few there were—were too high. I'd sit on the grassy area outside the building and think about how there had to be a way to be close to her all the time. She was left out of the information chain in that she had so little 'story' of her family or origin, and even less truth. And there was I, in a similar position—was I a novice guide? It didn't seem I could be inside buildings with her in the way I walked beside her outside. And that was just the start of what I wanted. I wanted Teresa to know about me, for then she would know more about life.

I knew we were on a journey together. I had to trust that there was some order to it all. When I slept, I'd dream that there would be a time she would wake and we could talk with each other but, until then, perhaps it was wise that I couldn't just show myself—after all, strong as she was, my showing up in a physical form would surely scare the hell out of her—no matter how strong, resilient, and tough she was. My dreams were also filled with projection—I had to be there to protect her… kind of like a bodyguard.

Not the Same Room as Him

The earliest memory I have of Tim is that of my family preparing Little Blue for Tim's visit. The dearest son coming home with his wife and kids for a summer visit straight from the Marine Corps in South Carolina to Minnesota.

Mom would be washing dishes and doing laundry to give the effect that it was always that way. She'd brown hamburger, cut onions, and boil rice to make one of Tim's favorite dishes, Spanish rice. Out in the garage fishing line was being placed into the fishing rods, worms were being stored in the fridge, and Dad was washing and waxing the boat. Tim's arrival was a big hoopla in our house.

I never had a memory of Tim until this day, yet it is such a vivid one.

Tim pulled onto the driveway wife and kids in tow. Mom and Dad so happy to see him—lots of hugs for Tim and his family as they unloaded themselves from the vehicle. I recall Dad hopping into action, helping with suitcases and the kids' toys. Mom and Tim's wife went quickly into the kitchen to finish up dinner while Dad and Tim headed to the garage—presumably to talk about fishing and hunting.

What brought great attention to this day was the cooler that had been in the back of Tim's vehicle and which, not long after they'd arrived, Tim had pulled out and placed on the picnic table in the yard. When he opened it, Dad was demonstrably excited—the excitement and disbelief of Tim's surprise in the cooler had everyone giggling and all the kids running around outside. Inside the cooler was a little shark. Tim had brought it straight from the ocean off South Carolina to be put on the dinner table as a treat for Dad.

The family ate and talked while the kids played on the freshly cut grass. Mom and Tim's wife chatted while cleaning up the kitchen. Tim and Dad continued catching up in the garage.

It was a happy day when I witnessed so much fuss for one family, and a back-and-forth enjoyment by all.

Not long after that visit, Tim and his family moved back to Minnesota. The dark side of this move was my noticing that Tim's expectations were that he be recognized as superior to all.

I was quite young—just a child—but what struck me was Tim's need to boast about all his achievements that didn't really seem like achievements to me. I agree serving in the Marine Corps (pronounced core) for a long time is an achievement, but this isn't what he was boasting about. What I saw was his being preoccupied with fantasies of success. False fantasies at that. He bought an old, rundown house that Dad would spend his days off helping Tim to fix. That or they'd be out fishing and hunting together, building deer stands, or cleaning their guns together.

Because our family didn't 'talk' about things, I was alone in my thoughts and opinions about Tim.

When he got a job in our small town as a cook, he called himself the chef. His exaggerated talents only made him more self involved, and his fantasies have brought me to the opinion that he had and has narcissistic tendencies. I often wondered if his role in the Marines changed him or enhanced an already self-centered personality. Perhaps, as a Marine, Tim was told how the public perceived Marines to be perfect and he took that on and expected to be told that by civilians, including family.

Due to our age difference, my only interactions were at family gatherings or if I was at his house playing with his children. But what haunts me to this day was Tim's betrayal when I was seventeen, determined to better myself and my situation.

TAKE AWAYS
ONE

Do not be afraid to make choices and take a stand when negotiating family or workplace social engagements.

TWO

Know the difference between ego and confidence—in yourself and in others. When someone is confident, they have firm trust in themselves; when someone is egotistical they present with self-importance.

The Many Spaces of Shelly

I knew her as Shelly, the girl who ran off to join the circus.

It was an odd way to refer to someone, but Mom and Dad said it, so I believed it.

And then, one day, the circus of Shelly came to town and set up in an apartment behind the schools, not far from Little Blue.

She always seemed nice when she visited.

On one of these occasions, it was matter-of-factly put in the conversation that Shelly was my biological mother. No mention of my adoption or the details of my arrival were given. It was simply a mention in passing, as if I could then just meld into the knowing what everyone else had always known. It was delivered in a way that I could absorb the secret without any emotional impact.

I have no recollection of a 'sit down and here's some important information'. One day she was Shelly, and the next day she was Shelly-is-the-daughter-of-Carol-and-Gary-and-she-happened-to-give-birth-to-you.

I tucked the information inside me beside a 'these people you are living with are your grandparents, your siblings are your aunts and uncles', and 'which people in your life knew this when they looked at you and had never said a word?'

I began going over to her place to see her—I was around twelve. There was never a mother/daughter relationship. Her behavior was no different than a sibling. Even when I went over, it never occurred to me that she was my mother—I still hadn't put it all together even though I'd been told. But that makes sense as there was no analysis that came with the news being delivered to me, nor did I receive any counselling.

I still lived with the people who had raised me: Mom and Dad.

I'd head over to Shelly's apartment when I was bored. She had a live-in boyfriend from Washington State who seemed to be nice, and she had a little girl who was a toddler who called Shelly 'mom'.

There was no status change between those I called my brothers and sisters—no switch to auntie and uncle. But the whole big-lie made a massive difference to the deepest parts of me.

Shelly's stay in Detroit Lakes didn't last long. She moved to Washington State with her boyfriend. Her life was basically a drama 'to be continued'.

Her ever-changing, stay tuned for the next dramatic episode, was a part of all our lives.

She remained Shelly. My grandparents remained Mom and Dad.

Full circle to the girl who ran away to the circus. That label didn't help Shelly. For that reason and others, Shelly couldn't seem to help Shelly either. There is so much more to her story, a part of which overlaps mine and which I can share from my perspective, and a part of it that is wholly her own.

TAKE AWAYS
ONE

Words matter.

TWO

Labels do not help anyone.
Watch your own conduct when you create or join with others
in continually calling someone by any name
(whether it elevates them to an expert
or it devalues them as in stupid)
all names impact limits, and power the formation of the belief
system.

Empty Rooms

When I was in grade four, the perfect age for a career to impress a child, a policeman called Officer E came to our school. He even brought a police dog with him. He came to our classroom to speak to students about drug abuse and present a form of 'just say no' campaign. It was called DARE, Drug Abuse Resistance Education. Immediately, I was struck by his blue uniform, the way he wore it, the way he carried himself, and his obvious passion for policing. From the moment Officer E began his presentation, I wanted to be part of that world; everything he represented spoke to the deepest parts of my heart.

I was at a point too, where I needed connection to stability. That strength imprinted on me and never left, despite all the stages that would follow. During elementary school, I'd often see Officer E and his police dog. I'd always run up to him and ask him questions. And I loved it when he did the K9 demonstrations.

When I was older, there was less enthusiasm when I ran into Officer E. In my teenage years, especially when I was in high school, he chased me around the city for skipping school, wrote many citations for being a minor consuming alcohol, and busted a lot of parties I attended.

The interesting thing is, my admiration of him never disappeared. I'd take my citation to court, and deal with it—no animosity toward Officer E.

I was alone a lot. Mom would work the swing shift, so she'd be gone when I got home from school and arrive home when I was in bed. Dad would sleep in the day and work all night. I was alone.

The carefree child who spent days at the waterslide, who loved to go to the library and read, and who had previously and regularly visited the place she called the Golden Paradise where her sister lived, was now 'more stuck' with two people who seemed either to be sleeping or working. They provided space and food and exampled hard work—but also created the perfect storm for a lonely teenager.

The teenager who had wanted her Mom and Dad to have attended her track meets—where she performed amazingly—was seemingly unwanted, an inconvenience, and a duty. She had stopped competing. Whether that perception was incorrect was not up for debate—a teenager's mind decides how something is, and then goes with it. Where there is dullness, there is rebellion and the need to find light.

I was lonely.

It was dark.

I needed to find other people.

I had to start looking for some light.

TAKE AWAYS
ONE

Children receive career downloads.
They meet someone or see a character on television who they
view as a hero,

then they develop a kinship of sorts
and can grow from seeing themselves in the same role as that
'hero'.

TWO

Children need heroes in their life.

Dangerous Rooms: I

When I was around fourteen, Shelly lived in Washington State; she'd not been in Minnesota for a long time. We'd been having semi-regular phone calls. Shelly talked about how great life was in Spokane. She told me that I could come out there and live with her. She went on about all the things I could see and do if I was there.

I was intrigued and wanted to go.

But I knew that Mom and Dad had severed their relationship with Shelly. Something had happened when she'd 'come back home' and taken an apartment. Since then, they'd ended all communication with her.

Back then I didn't know what it was. I still don't, but can make an educated guess that she had come home to get her life together, they had helped her out—financially—and then she'd not followed through.

It was the beginning of my rebellion years. I wanted to do whatever I wanted. I told Shelly I wanted to move out and be with her and her boyfriend and my half-sister, Naomi.

Shelly said she was thrilled.

I knew I was hanging with the wrong people in my home-town; I just wanted to fit in, to have people care about me and be involved with me. I hoped that going to Spokane would give me a support system that was not made up of the wrong people.

I saved a couple paychecks from my part time job so that a friend could purchase me a one-way Greyhound ticket from Detroit Lakes to Spokane, a trip that would take many hours.

With Dad sleeping in the evenings and Mom working until eleven-thirty at night, my exit was easy. I packed a bag and left the house without them knowing.

I remember boarding the bus and wondering if I was making the worst decision of my life. But I also convinced myself that Mom and Dad did not want me around.

I desperately wanted to feel wanted, loved, needed, and valued. I knew I did not feel that way where I was living, nor had I ever. I wanted more from my family.

I found a seat next to a younger male, then settled in for the trip. With my hoodie pulled up we began the trip west. Sometime through the trip the male and I began talking and I told him that I was running away and going to live with my biological mom in Spokane. He promised not to tell anyone. We chatted back and forth. Later the next night, in the middle of the night, the guy I was sitting next to woke me and alerted me to the police officer in the aisle. I realized the bus had been pulled over. My seatmate told me to pretend I was sleeping, and to keep the hood of my hoodie over my head. I peaked a couple of times as the officer made his way up the aisle toward the back where I was sitting. When the officer was close, I shut my eyes and made sure my head was on the shoulder of my seatmate.

It wasn't good enough for the Montana State Trooper who shook me 'awake', and asked where I was going and who I was with.

I explained I was going to Washington, and I was with the guy next to me. The guy nodded and the Trooper turned and went to the front of the bus. I breathed a sigh of relief.

Next thing I knew, the officer had turned around and approached me again. He asked if my name was Teresa.

I began to cry.

He told me that my parents just wanted to make sure I was safe, and to know where I was going. I told him I was safe, and I was going to stay with Shelly. The Trooper then got on his police radio. "We have her," he said.

A few seconds later the voice at the other end said, "Her parents said she can go."

That was it. They'd noticed after more than a day that I'd gone, checked things out, and then made the decision to let me go. Was that a tough decision for them? I like to think so. Had they folded? Was I another family casualty because of their exhaustion, or simply an extension of some kind of tough love blended with old-fashioned, non-emotional parenting.

Two things were for sure:

1. They didn't understand I needed love and validation because they didn't know how that worked in a healthy parenting relationship.
2. I was on my way to Spokane.

TAKE AWAYS
ONE

Mindfulness gifts us the headspace we need so that we know our feelings are temporary; they come and go—therefore, we don't need to attach or identify with those feelings.

TWO

Our ability to exercise patience and understanding with those who have
abused us, neglected us, and betrayed us
is a superpower of sorts.

Dangerous Rooms: II

My arrival in Spokane was underwhelming. Nothing special. No welcoming crew. No fanfare. Yet I was excited to be there and see what was next for me.

The strange thing is, I wasn't taken to stay with Shelly and her boyfriend and my half-sister. I was taken to Shelly's friend's house (who also had a daughter). I was told Shelly was in the process of moving, so this was best.

I quickly became friends with Shelly's friend's daughter. When Shelly and her boyfriend and my half-sister moved, I went to stay with them. Besides going to school, my role was to look after my younger half-sister, clean up the dog-poop in the yard, and cook dinners while Shelly 'rehearsed'.

There were no activities that Shelly had talked about on the phone. It mattered but it didn't because I just wanted to be loved and valued. I wanted to be validated as a nice person. I wanted a family. I went along with her requests.

Shelly did not behave as a parent; she'd be in her room dancing provocatively to heavy metal music, then suddenly invite me in to show me all her moves. Her boyfriend would be in the living room, smoking tobacco from a pipe. His brother was staying with them; his behavior was weird, but I later understood he had been completely strung out on drugs. I'd never used drugs. I didn't know what that looked like.

A lot of people came and went from Shelly and her boyfriend's place.

As time went on, Shelly's behavior became extreme. One occasion, when I was on my monthly cycle and asked Shelly if she had a tampon, her immediate reaction was to flip out and say that I wasn't a virgin. She asked me who'd I'd had sex with—I didn't even know what sex was. She yelled and stomped around the house accusing me of lying. "Only people who have had sex can wear tampons," she screamed. She demanded I tell her the truth, and then dragged me to the living room and asked her boyfriend to verify that a girl could only use tampons if they'd had sex. And he backed up her ridiculous statement. She flew into a rage, interrogating me as to the identity of the person I'd had sex with.

I kept telling I hadn't done anything with any boy. There was no boy.

She sent me to my room for not telling her the truth. The next day I was given sanitary pads for my period.

Though I registered in school when I arrived in Spokane, my attendance there was short-lived, and not because I skipped. One fall afternoon, Shelly and Roy asked me to rake the leaves in the back yard. I spent a lot of time out there working for them, cleaning up the yard and, on this occasion, I got all the leaves into a big pile. When I was done, Shelly inspected my job and flipped out again. She flew into another rage and wouldn't stop screaming. She said I needed to rake all the leaves in the back yard. I was upset and yelled back that I had done that. Then she showed me there were leaves stuck in the metal fence between the yard and the neighbor's yard.

I refused.

She sent me to my room and told me I was not allowed to come out.

Within a day or two, Shelly had made a plan that was completely despicable—how she managed it, I'm not sure. I was taken to some type of group home or rehabilitation center. When I arrived, I was kept in one of those 'white-walled' rooms they feature on television shows that have characters who are locked away for mental health reasons. At the 'home' I was given a chore list, and I attended school through them at their facility.

I had no idea what was happening and why I was there. Nothing that Shelly had promised on the phone calls was happening. I was in a nightmare. Shelly had found a way to commit me to some kind of facility, and I was clearly without anyone to love or nurture me.

I was terrified.

I was able to think things through and get in touch with some new friends I'd met at the new school in Spokane. I then managed to call Shelly's friend that I'd stayed with when I'd first moved to Spokane.

I told her what was happening, and she came and picked me up. I hid out at her house until she could save up enough money to get me a bus ticket back home.

The more I thought about it, the more I could see my role was to serve Shelly, and I realized that her provocative dancing was that of an adult entertainer in what most people know as strip clubs.

I called Mom and Dad in Minnesota and told them what was happening. I apologized and said that I was going to come home. I asked them not to tell Shelly as she would not allow it to happen if she found out where I was.

The thing is, Shelly did come over to her friend's house to look for me. One time I hid under the bed, another time in a closet. What child in her early teens deserves this? How can this happen? I saw it all as part of my 'normal' life at the time. In later years I'd see how it is 'normal' for many families I encountered in my work. Sometimes that felt like I was looking into a mirror or walking into a scene from my own past.

Eventually, Shelly's friend paid for my bus ticket, and I was able to make it out of Washington State. No, Mom and Dad didn't send the money; they never mentioned the facility and escape.

I profusely thanked Shelly's friend for saving my life. If it wasn't for her stepping up, I don't know where I would be today. Back then I could count on one hand how many people I felt cared about me. This person was one of those. I hardly new her in terms of the time I knew her, yet she was a guardian angel. She felt compassion for me. She didn't let dysfunction get swept under the carpet.

Inside, I told myself: "I will never be Shelly."

I later learned that Shelly was a drug addict and a stripper when I had been in Spokane. When she'd locked herself in her room she'd been strung out like her boyfriend Roy's brother. I have no idea if her boyfriend used.

It's obvious to me now that there were drugs moving through that house—I suspect Shelly used more than she sold. I realize this may appear as a terrible thing to say about one's parent, but it is also more terrible to know that children—my half-sister and I—were exposed to Shelly's dangerous lifestyle.

In contrast to Shelly's dysfunctional and abusive ways, I can express some compassion for her situation. I was not in her shoes. I was not aware of what she had gone through in her early years. I could identify with her needs, as a child, perhaps not being met in the way of feeling loved and valued. She was always referred to as the girl who ran away to join the circus.

I don't know if Shelly was genetically predisposed to drug addiction but, if she was, it's unlikely there'd have been any intervention or family counseling.

It was a long time before I spoke to Shelly. What she did was abusive and inexcusable. What she did next affected my half-sister, Naomi: she left her with her boyfriend and went to another state with a guy who was much younger than her. In essence, she left her child with a known drug dealer and moved across the country. I will never understand this, even though I have since been told the reason—and it doesn't make sense to me.

Shelly left the younger guy and was gone again. She did not resurface for at least ten years. When she did, she was in another relationship. She eventually reconnected with Naomi,

This story is shared not for pity; if anything it is humiliating to put it out there. I tell this story because this is a prime example of what and who I was determined not to be as a parent.

At the time of writing, I can share that, over the last decade, Shelly has lived less than two hours from my daughter and me; I've seen her fewer than five times. In my entire life, I've never received a birthday card from her, nor has my daughter (her granddaughter). I have often wished it could have been different—wished that on occasions, such as my graduating college for the first time, or from the police academy, that she would be there... proud of me. But that is all it ever has been: a wish.

Now, later in her life, Shelly appears to be drug and alcohol free, and is in a relationship. However, she still finds it hard to take on the role of parent. When there is a crisis in Shelly's life, I will often be contacted to help out. When one of my half-sisters, Naomi, reached out to her to ask for help with her own addiction issues, Shelly could not bring herself to be there. At that particular time, I shared my feelings about her selfishness, and my views on the duty of a parent. I ranted and became emotional, trying to make the point of how 'this reaching out of her daughter' would be the perfect opportunity for a sober couple—Shelly and her long-term guy—to help. Sadly, Shelly countered my suggestions with an excuse of why she could not help.

Over time, I have realized why more than one person in my family has completely cut contact with Shelly. I try hard to understand the way Shelly functions; I've decided that she has not matured, and operates the way a young child might. I tell myself her mental capacity cannot comprehend the dynamics of family connection and affection that come through responsibility and respect. Even in a sober state, and over fifty, she doesn't get it. At the time of editing this manuscript, and seemingly in recovery, Shelly has not come to terms with the events of the past.

My take on my own situation is this: each person I called my siblings have their own stories—and there is bound to be both heartbreak and joy in them. There are lessons in all of our stories. To learn from them, a person must find their truth in those stories, and then choose whether they want to apply compassion and forgiveness of others and of self.

TAKE AWAYS
ONE

Lessons are repeated until learned.

Notice that through those 'been there done that' before moments.

TWO

The hardest part of all relationships is balance:
To not cross over into being used,
and to not be so hypervigilant that we become fearful.

Hyena

There never was any heart truly great and generous,
that was not also tender and compassionate.
—Robert Frost

*It's really hard to be compassionate sometimes, even when you are
an animal guide—well, it was for me. I knew what compassion
was—and I could explain it—but I had a hard time getting into
compassion-mode when it came to feeling it for some of the people
involved with My Teresa. I know it's not all 'spiritual-high-selflike'
but it's true. It was just so hard to understand why certain things
were done around Teresa and to Teresa.*

*Let's start with the loneliness that turned into action that turned
into a cross-country bus trip.*

*For a long time, Teresa had needed the kind of support that all
children need. As she began to feel all the feels inside her maturing-
self, she experienced more loneliness than ever before. When she
made the decision to leave, I started to fear for more than just her
general safety; I was terrified for her earthly life.*

*When she came out of the house with a packed bag, I knew where
she was going. I knew it was a long way away. When she got into
the car, I raced behind that car and, when it stopped at stop signs, I
ran ahead because I knew she was going to take a bus—and I knew*

I could not run across the country and keep up with it. This meant I got there ahead of her and worked on a plan to see how to get onto the bus. I had to figure out how to lay low and cross some kind of an ethereal barrier to be in a 'place', albeit a bus where she was.

I was at her ankles when she climbed onto the bus. I tried to slink up the steps that led passengers to their seats that sat above the large storage area that was accessed separately below. I was met with an invisible barrier when she hit the second step. I'm ashamed to say I even nipped at her ankle, to get her to see me, but she just zombied up the steps and disappeared to the left once she reached the driver. I tried again, slinking lower and slipping between the legs of other passengers. No, dice. It was time for plan B.

The underside of the bus offered some kind of portal, because I simply sniffed my way along the underside of the vehicle then jumped up to the cargo hold and planted myself on a soft-sided piece of luggage. I was in. I set about envisioning her sitting beside someone safe. Then I focused on the seeds needed to grow some safety at the other end.

Shelly was a tough person to plant seeds around. I could not break through to her no matter what other energy I accessed. She faced so many challenges, as she always had. While I'd always sent Shelly positive energy, I could not break through to her. I switched my intentions to someone in Shelly's life who could and would step forward in compassion. When I'd done that, I sang vibrational lullabies to Teresa. There were miles and miles to go before she faced her next challenge. She needed to rest.

And then we were stopped, way before the destination. I found my hyena-self standing at the bottom of the opened stair of the bus door, right behind the boots of a law enforcement officer. Teresa's little heart was just beating so fast that I could barely breathe my earth breaths.

I yelled from the side of the highway: "Someone, just love this little girl. Love her completely and fully. Understand her."

I'm sorry, but sacred or spiritual as thought guides and guardian angels are, I was not the perfect model of forgiveness, nor was I wholly compassionate toward those in Teresa's life. Then I scrambled back to the luggage storage compartment as the bus began to rumble down the highway with Teresa still on it. Carol and Gary knew where she was. And that was enough for them. It was the best way they could deal with the situation. Teresa would continue on to where Shelly lived. Seriously, there were times when I wanted to tear some family members limb from limb. I'm just being honest here. I was young and didn't know the full powers of compassion and forgiveness. I was learning.

I ran behind the car when we arrived in the west. And I sat in the back yard of the house of chaos. Again, I was a novice guardian; I hadn't learned the rules, but I knew that I wanted to break them when I saw the horrible things that Shelly asked of Teresa, and when I heard the way she spoke. I had no idea where to turn when I saw the drug use in that home and the drug users who visited it. There was a ridiculousness to it all, and Teresa just wanted to be loved.

"I love you, Teresa," I howled at the Washington moon: "You are my everything." But it wasn't enough. Teresa wanted love from Shelly. Shelly didn't know how to love Teresa. If I stretch past my agenda, I will say Shelly didn't know how to love completely and deeply and unconditionally. It was heartbreaking.

There were moments that I truly believed I should not be a hyena, or a guide, because I did not have the strength to witness what was happening right in front of me.

And then it got worse. Teresa was brave and advocated for herself, Shelly took retribution by sending her to a secure facility. And that is when I was able to—for some magical reason—get inside. Maybe because it was secure and she wasn't allowed out, or maybe I'd served a certain time in service; it can't be because I was good at my job because I was no longer the peaceful, patient guide; I was bitter and angry at the time. It unsettled me about my role—how could I be a higher power when I was so upset. I wasn't violent, I was incensed at the injustice of it all, and angry with Carol and Gary for letting down Teresa. I was livid with Shelly. Absofuckinglutely batshit infuriated. Maybe that's where it cracked. Maybe that's what brought on the power to breach the building and go be with Teresa. Maybe we have to have times of extreme emotions to push us into our gifts and get us back on the road to being passionate about a cause.

The positive was I could sleep at the bottom of her bed. And some nights I could inch up to where she curled into her sadness, and I could nuzzle her tear-streaked face. And I was closer to getting into her head and making a plan. This helped the anger subside and helped me find the helpers.

What was happening outside the secure building was that the seeds that I'd planted with the person who had more kindness than I did—the person who had befriended Shelly—started to grow. Teresa's strength and resilience kicked into high gear. She was empowered to get someone to make a call for her. And then that person, Shelly's 'friend', came and took Teresa away from the horrible place—and ultimately freed her from Shelly's distorted views and unparalleled negativity and power. That person brought Teresa to her own little home. She did not take her back to Shelly.

And that is when I started to understand compassion more. In the calmer times while Teresa was with that friend—even hiding from Shelly—I had time to put that anger aside. Sure, I still couldn't understand why Carol and Gary couldn't just send a plane ticket to

Teresa and show their love in that way, but I did take some time to do a compassion refresher and then an advanced course.

In the opening lines of the ethereal classroom, I learned that Compati is the Latin word behind the word the English-speaking world knows as compassion. Compati means to suffer with.

But I thought to myself that, today, we don't look at it as 'to suffer with'. Today, we define it as understanding someone else's suffering, and offering comfort. Compassion is exampled through kind words, friendly gestures, or longer-term conversations with actions and outcomes that help the one who is suffering.

What I realized for myself is the power in compassion is being able to connect. Connection is what helps groups go beyond survival and thrive. Hyenas do that. So do members of a tribe who genuinely care about each other.

I strayed from the lecture and thought about what the opposite of compassion was and right away I saw a vision of the human world, and people turning away from each other. Some were doing that by ignoring those in need, others were even praying upon those in need, and taking advantage of them. I woke up and paid attention to a spirit wiser than me. They said that compassion is an act of love, a solution, and a practice, and that those who are compassionate benefit within themselves through the goodness they create.

I knew then that it would take a lot of strength and patience for me to see the situations of Shelly, and of Carol and Gary, so that I could understand their limitations and suffering too. This would be difficult because I was assigned to Teresa. To guide her. How could I guide her if I was on their side? I wanted only to be on her side.

A cloud of knowledge pulled me in and absorbed me, then filled me up with its contents. I could learn to identify the feelings of others as well as Teresa, and then guide her through the difficulties created by the suffering of others and help her develop boundaries *rather than the 'hate' and 'rage' I was seemingly moving toward. I could feel the pain of others rather than react to it to protect My Teresa. I could stand by and listen to their stories, and then offer calm visions to the best of my ability, while upholding my sacred contract with My Teresa.*

When the lesson was finished, I signed up for forgiveness 101, and then curled up near Teresa as she waited—gratefully, I might add—for Shelly's 'friend' to save the money for Teresa to take a bus back to Minnesota, I watched that friend's karma account increase one-hundredfold in her karma-bank-balance.

No Room

I don't remember the reception I received after I traveled all the way back to Detroit Lakes. That not remembering most likely reflects that there was no welcoming committee at Little Blue. Mom and Dad would have been going through the motions that they had been playing out for decades. When I was born, they'd stepped up and raised me when Shelly couldn't or wouldn't, and now they were doing a form of that again. Stepping in, providing a place to stay, and food. Never any sitting and talking—always on the other side of nurture.

As I looked for a place to fit in, I began hanging with others who had previously looked for a place to fit in and formed a group. I didn't want to be lonely.

I wanted to feel valued. I wanted to be recognized. I needed emotional connection. I needed love. I needed validation for who I was.

I started to hang out a little bit with a group of kids who seemed to like me. I liked them because they filled the needs I had.

I didn't feel lonely.

Some of the kids were much older than me.

I only felt lonely at home in Little Blue.

And that had continued when I was in Spokane—the lonely feeling.

And on my return to Detroit Lakes.

And then that changed, and Mom and Dad announced that we'd be moving.

Even moving was done without any pre-talk. It just came to be that the green house down the street was going to be where Mom and Dad lived and, by virtue of me living with them, I would be going there too.

Little Blue would forever be the house at the top of the hill of a dead-end street, a house where my foundation resided, a house steps from the big woods. The move a few houses down the hill to a small green house just simply happened—no fanfare, no chatter about it, a 'that's where we're going to be living, that's your bedroom.'

I do not remember any For Sale signs, packing, or a moving truck. Suddenly, we were three people living in a smaller place that had its bedrooms upstairs.

I was lonely there too.

TAKE AWAYS
ONE

Every person deserves to be valued.

TWO

Whenever you can genuinely acknowledge another person, you change their life.

Hyena

Home is the place where, when you have to go there, they have to take you in.
—Robert Frost

The African savanna is essentially a large home where each creature and plant feels a deep belonging. Sometimes it is a wild and chaotic place, and there are problems like storms or droughts, but every creature and plant knows inside themself that this is where they belong. Those who live there, in all forms, and the visiting rains and beams of sunlight are all so comfortable in their place that they fit together into a community. That is what makes it a sacred place... the knowing of the belonging.

All homes should be sacred places—tents, caves, apartments, houses, where people fit together—where they bring the whole of themselves into a group to make a nucleus of love; where they form a hub from which the dwelling and its occupants become a home.

Little Blue was a place that held a family in distress for many years. It was a house. There was a family in it. But it was not enough for Teresa. It had held the loving hearts of Carol and Gary, but it could not change their stoic ways. Teresa wanted a home. She needed a sense of belonging to a group where all the people under the roof could support and understand each other even when things were difficult. Especially when they were difficult.

When she didn't get that feeling in the deepest part of her, she was compelled, without even knowing, to search for where she belonged. I could identify because in my role as a guide from another world, and with a connection to my sisterhood of hyenas on the savanna, I was learning the ropes of belonging as well, though I knew in my heart of hearts that I was deeply accepted in the house of humanity, in a universal family of loving beings. I was just new to this universal home.

When Teresa began to look for another home, even though she didn't know she was looking, she left Little Blue and headed to Spokane. But she didn't find a home in Spokane; there was only danger and heartbreak.

A Metal Garage

My group of friends still included a shady crew of people—I was still looking for love but didn't know that. I was responding to a set of needs we all have, and the group I found provided what I needed. When I was with them, I was cool and in the clique.

I began staying out at night. I'd attend parties with them. I'd follow them anywhere, and even chase them. I needed to be sated by their attention, and I was willing to take the habits that came along with it all—though I hadn't used any drugs at this time.

One night, the group was going from party to party, and decided to walk to the next one. We were responsible degenerates; we walked—no one had stolen their parents' vehicle to joyride.

It was that time of year when fall has bled its icy nights into winter. It was ten o'clock cold, and we all wore winter jackets and gloves, blowing smoke from our cigarettes and watching it mix with our visible breaths in the freezing air around us.

Suddenly, headlights mixed with flashing red and blue headed toward us. "Oh, shit. It's the cops," said a friend. The friend took off running. I was confused because I had never run from the cops and, even though I had a pack of cigarettes on me and had a couple drinks inside me, I didn't think it warranted running. My thought was that, if I played it cool, they would stop and ask what we were doing and, at the most, send us home. Four more friends began to run. I continued to walk. Then the police car flew past me, taking off after the five friends who were running.

When they passed me, I panicked, chucked the pack of smokes into someone's yard, and ran. Why I ran I did not know. But I ran and ran and ran. I ran through backyards until I slowed and looked for cover. The crunching of hard snow alerted me. Then there was a voice, louder than a whisper, like a soft yell. "Teresa."

It was one of my friends. They said, 'Keep running. As fast as you can." And so, I did. I'd done a lot of cross country in track and field at school and the running came easy. I ran so fast and hard I didn't even know where I was until, splash!

I ran right into a flowing river. The water was so cold it took my breath away. The current was difficult to fight. I was carried downstream for a bit; my jacket became saturated and heavy.

I was able to grab an overhanging tree branch and slowly pull my shivering body out.

My friend had gone into the river too and managed to get out. Back on solid ground, shivering and scared, I did not know where to go or what to do.

The night sky was illuminated with police lights from numerous vehicles. Then I recognized the ferocious barking of the K9 unit. Officer E called out, "Come out or I'm sending in the dog."

Frantic, and not even understanding what I was doing or why I even ran, I knew I needed to finish what I started. Even with the heavy clothes, and the adrenaline, I continued in escape mode. A red, metal garage and a large, downed tree came into view. My friend was running alongside and indicated to move away from the river. I headed for the garage and tree. I thought, if I could lie quietly between the two, the dog and Officer E would not see me. The plan was that I'd make my way home after that.

I slowed my breathing so as not to produce a cloud. Boots crunching a top layer of snow-ice broke near me. A flashlight shone all around, back and forth over the area where I was lying. The crunching got louder and the barking too. I closed my eyes and took a deep breath so I could hold it for a moment in time. This was the biggest mistake of my entire evening, well, beside the fact that I ran. As I took the deep breath and closed my eyes the movement from my body moved a branch under me and rubbed against the metal garage.

"Don't fucking move." Officer E's voice was accompanied by growling and barking.

I opened my eyes to a blinding light. The commands to exit from behind the fallen tree continued as I tried to move branches so that I could follow the instructions. The police dog kept growling a message that he wanted to rip my throat out.

I finally managed to pry my way out from behind the tree with my hands up, apologizing for what I'd done, though prior to running I'd not really done anything other than walk to a party.

My hands were still up. I was shivering from fear and the severe cold, dripping wet and pissed off with myself.

Another officer handcuffed me and put me in the back seat of a warm squad car. I was happy not to be frozen, even though I was caught.

I knew I was done. My Dad would surely whoop my ass.

I was going to feel the wrath for weeks if not months. As the officer walked away, a voice came from the front seat. "Teresa, they got your ass too?" In the front seat of the squad car was the buddy who'd gone for the late-night float in the freezing river with me.

"Want to see something?" said my friend. He began to wiggle around in the front seat of the squad car. He kept it up, moving at different angles, Suddenly, he threw his cuffed hands in the air. He'd managed to wiggle into a freedom that he could operate from. "I'm out of here," he said. He opened the squad car door and exited, then tried to open my back door but it wouldn't open. He took off running, still handcuffed.

I recall that moment, wet and cold, but at least not freezing and in a river. My thoughts were specifically, 'What the fuck is happening? This guy was caught, has now escaped, and is running down the street still handcuffed.'

I accepted my fate. I was caught, I was done. I was in a lot of trouble for running from the police.

Then Officer E showed up in the driver's seat. "Hey, where did the guy go?"

"Straight ahead and to the left," I said.

"So, that means straight and to the right," he said. His message on the radio repeated the direction, while I became upset with myself for giving away the direction of my friend.

We drove in the direction of Little Blue, up the hill on the street that ended where the forest started. But we stopped at the green house. My old and new address was known to more officers than Officer E. First, Dad had once been a County Deputy; second, I'd been brought home before. But nothing like this.

When Officer E questioned about why I ran, I told him I had no idea. He dropped me off at home and said, your Dad's punishment for you will be far worse than what the police can do. We'll let him deal with you.

Dad had already left for work at the time I was dropped at home; Mom had arrived home at eleven-thirty from her swing shift and was at the kitchen table when I walked in. I sure got a verbal ass-beating from her, but she saved me from a sore behind or worse: being put out on the street.

I changed into dry clothes and waited until after Mom had gone to bed. When I was comfortable she was sleeping, I headed out to check if my friend had gotten home from his adventure—they only lived a couple of blocks away. I hoped the group could come back together.

I held the back door's handle in a way that it wouldn't loudly click shut. Baby steps across the porch, then creeping slowly down the driveway—eyes out for the police. Once I was satisfied that it was me and the streetlights, I dashed down the street, cutting across in front of the streetlights, checking over my shoulder, and holding my breath each time I heard a car's engine.

The yelling reached me half a block from my friend's place. The front door was open, and the lights inside were so bright I could see into the house. A squad car was in the driveway.

Most people would have gone home. I approached the house, up the icy walkway to the front door. What I saw was straight out of a movie. Officer E held the feet of my friend. My friend was gripping the handle of the fridge door—which was wide open. Officer E was basically trying to drag my friend out, with or without the fridge.

My friend's mom and dad were yelling and screaming but I couldn't put their words together. Next thing, he was separated from the fridge and my friend's parents were able to help their son and slam the door on Officer E.

As Officer E knocked on the door, the parents shouted to come back with a warrant. At that point, with my friend's parents protecting their son, I knew I'd be okay for the rest of the night, unless Mom or Dad discovered I was gone.

Officer E seemed to have a soft spot in his heart for me. We would run into each other many more times in life.

TAKE AWAYS
ONE

Risk assessment is always required before jumping into certain situations.

TWO

Spontaneity is a wonderful thing…
But when it comes to life-changing decisions,
planning is essential.

.

The lay of the land

In the little town of Detroit Lakes there was a part we called 'the strip' The strip started up by what we called the mall. This mall wasn't a big one. It was and still is a big brown brick building containing a Pizza Hut, Dairy Queen, movie theatre, Claire's Jewelry store, and a Vanity clothing store. Vanity was the most important part of this mall because in the 90s it was the only place that offered clothing for teenagers and young women that was reasonably affordable.

On the corner across from the mall was the old Main Street café. It was the only café in the area with the best breakfast at the best prices. Their biscuits and gravy tasted homemade, and were my go-to breakfast when on a plate with bacon and eggs. A kid could sit there for hours with their cup of coffee, chat with their friends, and, of course, smoke their Marlboros.

Across the street from the café was a pet store.

If you started a tour of the strip from that brown-brick mall, you could head south down the strip—or main drag. All along the way were small stores: A quaint bookstore—the only bookstore in town. Across the street from the bookstore was a craft store. Then came Norbys, a high end, brand-name store. I remember walking through that store, daydreaming and wishing—daydreaming about getting Doc Martens, Calvin Klein shirts, and Tommy Hilfiger pants. I believed every other kid at school shopped there; just wanted to be able to fit in with them and wear the same clothes.

JC Pennys came next—it had been there since before I was born. Across from JC's was a high-end sporting goods and gun store. You could get anything for your outdoor activities and school sports. The sheriff's office was next door. Police cars constantly pulled in and out of this space.

Head a little further down the street, cross the road, and you'd come up on the public library. This was one of my favorite places to hang out when I was younger. I would go in, curl up with a book, and read all day. Upstairs was every teen magazine you could imagine, including Vogue and Seventeen. I enjoyed this because I didn't have subscriptions; Mom and Dad thought them unnecessary. Girls at school would bring them to school and pass them around in class and talk about them at lunch. I was never a part of that crowd, so I had to catch up on the free magazines at the library.

The library provided comfort and safety in my younger days. It allowed me to learn and explore anything I wanted. So perfect was it that, as an adult, I chose one of the study rooms to prepare for the police officer's exam.

If you can pull yourself away from the library, and head further south, you would find the hospital on one side and Becker Pet and Garden on the other. Becker's stocked dog and cat food, anything you might need for birds, and everything to do with gardens and gardening. It is the same place I would shop as an adult for my Great Danes' food.

A little further south featured a few restaurants, a dental office, and some gas stations.

Things started to get fun and interesting if you were to turn right at the next corner. One of my favorite childhood memories, and some of the best times, took place at Wild Waters waterslides. I may not have had teen magazine subscriptions, but Mom and Dad bought me a season pass to Wild Waters. I spent many hours sliding down the massive waterslide that zipped sliders into its chlorine-filled, bubbling pool below. I'd climb those stairs, one by one, holding the tube to go down the slide with. Then get onto the tube and hold on for dear life and scream with pure happiness all the way down. Then, I'd do it again. Sometimes, I'd race friends up the steps to the enclosed tube slide, and hours of happiness would speed by. When I got home from all that hot sun and sliding, I'd grab myself an ice-cream or a small snack.

Across the road from the slides was the large lake the town was named after. It could be seen from the waterslide—all the beach, the people on the beach, people playing in the water with their children, families playing catch, and dedicated sun-tanners in their bikinis bronzing their bodies.

Later in my teens, I'd be with people who had a car, and we'd roll past the beach—real slow—with music blaring. The lake ran parallel with the road for about three-quarters of a mile, then there was a turnaround area, and a cruiser could do the whole thing again but on the other side of the road. There were many late nights cruising the strip, listening to music and hanging out.

TAKE AWAYS
ONE

You are a map of your life.

TWO

You can get the lay of the land by taking a tour of your own situations.

The Fire Escape

Behind the brown brick mall was a white two-storey house. The front had the appearance of a beautiful home, yet it had been converted to a law office. At the back was a long staircase to a second-floor apartment. It was there I was introduced to a whole new world that changed my life forever; one without which I wouldn't be writing my book.

The first time I went up the staircase behind the beautiful white house conversion was with a friend who was much older than me. I was just sixteen and pretty naïve to the world of older teens. Even though my sisters—who were really my aunts—had pregnancies and babies, I was much younger than my years in any kind of knowledge about sex and drugs. I read teen magazines that showed clean-faced girls-next-door, and promoted lifestyles that involved getting high grades, wearing designer clothing, and supporting athletic ability (the latter which I had; I'd done well in track at school.)

I remember we were at my girlfriend Becky's house; it was a summer night. Her mother was at work. Somehow there was a decision that we should get some marijuana. I'd been hanging out with older kids, but hadn't tried pot. She said she knew where we'd go to get it, and she called a friend who drove us. I sat in the front seat, dancing in my seat to the hip-hop music that was bumping out the speakers. Becky was in the back doing the same. We pulled into an alleyway that I knew—one I saw all the time because it was behind the mall that was near to the waterslide. It was the beautiful two-storey home. When we turned into the alley, the driver lowered the music and turned out the headlights. I was immediately concerned, and asked my friend what was happening. She said it was all okay, it was what all people had to do.

We operated in silence, other than my friend whispering for me to follow. As we mounted the stairs, music seeped from the dark house. When we reached a platform filled with garbage, my friend knocked on the door. No one answered. She knocked again and again.

After about the fifth time, the music lowered and voices inside were shushing each other. Then someone brushed up against the other side of the door. My friend knocked again and said, 'Hey, it's me.'

The door slowly opened. A sickly-smoky-sweet aroma hit me. I followed my friend into the dimly lit apartment.

"This is my friend, Teresa. She's cool," she said.

My attention was on the layout of the tiny apartment. A little kitchen with a round table, garbage all over the floor, led to a small living room with a sofa and chair. A couple of older men—perhaps in their forties—were planted on the sofa. They each had long, greasy hair. One of them had a beard. I immediately registered I was the youngest person there.

All I remember them saying is, "Is she a cop, she a cop?"

I was terrified. I was a kid. All I could think was that this is how I will die. I'm going to be murdered by these old-ass drug dealers.

Becky reassured them I wasn't a cop and that I was only a 16-year-old girl that came with her to get some pot.

How they could have thought I was old enough to be a cop was a mystery to me—though it might have been based on their lack of any intelligence and that they were wasted.

I tried hard not to look like a scared little girl. One of the old, greasy-haired men pulled out a large Ziploc bag full of pot. He began to roll a few joints for my friend. Meanwhile, I was offered a beer—I have never liked beer—and you bet my scared little ass took that beer and I drank it. I think I did it because I was expected to, and I wanted to show them I wasn't a threat. I also thought it would calm me.

After the joints were rolled, which seemed like hours due to their testing me, and with my friend trying to get the pot for free, one of the greasy-haired men lit up a joint and passed it around.

I watched wide eyed because the only thing I had ever smoked were cigarettes. The music was turned up, and as I watched the joint travel around the room, I realized I could not see out the windows—tinfoil covered every inch of glass. Laughter erupted between the others, and then the joint came to me. I politely said no thanks and tried to pass it to the person next to me.

What I quickly learned about the world of drugs and buying drugs is never to go into a drug dealers house and turn down the drugs that are going around.

The demeanor of everyone changed in the instant I said no thank you.

"She is a fucking cop," said one of the old men.

I tried to explain that I wasn't a cop, I'd just never smoked pot before.

"I just came here with my friend," I said.

I was told that I needed to smoke the pot before I was able to leave. To make sure I wouldn't ruin my friend's friendship with these people, and possibly to save my life, I took a hit of the pot.

I began coughing profusely. my eyes watering. Everyone in the room began to laugh hysterically.

One of the men there said that they were just fucking with me. They knew I wasn't a cop.

A short time later a younger male came out of a side room and asked about all the commotion. As I sat there in silence—still a little scared—I looked at him as they told him my story. He grabbed a beer and joint and joined their laughter generated by the story of my taking my first hit of a joint. He looked at me—beer in his hand and a joint in his mouth—and smiled and said, "My name is Nick."

The night turned into the early morning hours, my friend and I listening to old-man stories and talking shit with Nick… and drinking beer and smoking pot.

This evening in this location in the beautiful white house with the not so beautiful alley apartment would be the start to my teenage love story. Tragedy or biggest blessing, depending on how you look at things.

*****

Short story, in hindsight: I began looking for love and adventure in all the wrong places. In seemingly a heartbeat, I went from conservative teen to sixteen and with a different crowd. In all the years I'd lived in Little Blue, there had never been any talking about how my siblings had been through stuff that I needed to be cautious of. There didn't seem to be any parenting that favored self-awareness.

I'm not playing the victim, here. And I did take responsibility for my actions. I'm recounting what I remember, and what—by fact—is a line of kids that were housed and fed and schooled but, when they hit puberty, they were free to lose themselves in the darker side of small-town life where other adults could influence highly vulnerable adolescents.

Most of us take risks when we are young. Some of us are aware of the consequences and take the risk anyway, believing we are invincible. A teenage brain will do that. But some of us get involved in risky situations when we are naïve by way of not having been aware of what we're getting into. For others it will be a bit of both combined with simply not having the closeness within family, without having been guided.

I can only remember a couple of times when Mom or Dad found a pipe in my jacket. They gave me heck, and that was it. They didn't take it any further. They said little about my behavior or my absences that were becoming regular. They never asked. I just came and went.

As I met 'new' friends, including one who was a much older girl than me—and only knew how to be resilient rather than safe—those new friends introduced me to alcohol and marijuana.

TAKE AWAYS
ONE

No is a complete sentence.

TWO

No thank you works too.

Hyena

I should not be withheld but that some day
Into their vastness I should steal away,
Fearless of ever finding open land,
Or highway where the slow wheel pours the sand.
Into My Own – Robert Frost

Frost talks about the certainty of not being able to stop our growth.

My Teresa seemed to go from innocence to full-on rock-and-roll and high-risk behaviors quickly.

One moment she was reading books in the library or running track at school—doing well but filled with a sadness that no one was on the bleachers to see her—and the next moment she was getting in a car with older kids, going along with what they were doing. In both worlds were music, but that is all those worlds had in common.

Perhaps if someone had been on those bleachers. I mean, I was, but that didn't matter. She needed family there.

I tried to pull her back, but life had other ideas.

It seemed only weeks before that she'd been at the waterslide with her young friends, then she'd done lots of babysitting, and now she was being pulled in and getting into dangerous territory. I could see she was getting in over her head with older friends. She wanted to be accepted and liked by people—in a group. And she was incredibly likable. She was fun, she loved to dance. Now she wanted to share that fun. She wanted to be part of conversations and activities that made her feel that she belonged and was valued.

It was just as Frost expressed: there was no holding back time, no stopping for a while to think about the growing up that was going to happen. I was powerless against the calendar. I had feared for her. I continued to be fearful for her. And I was broken-hearted that I was not enough for her. She didn't want to run in nature with me, she wanted to be accepted and involved with real people.

Bedroom

Life evolved quickly after that visit to the second-floor apartment. A few weeks later, I was staying at the house of a man who was at least 35 years old. He was 'the guy' who had the party house in town. I'd met him through other friends. I was there so often that I had my own room there—a crash room after a night of drinking—at the top of the steepest, almost unclimbable, staircase. The house offered black lights on the walls, huge speakers blasting Biggie Smalls and Tupac, and a living room that was essentially a dance floor. People didn't only go for the dancing—there was free alcohol and drugs for anyone who wanted them.

After all night benders, the owner of the house would cook for anyone who'd stayed there a breakfast of steak and eggs, or anything they wanted.

I'd be there almost every Thursday through Sunday. Every week, new people would show up. The music would change. I loved the music. I had always loved music and dancing. The menu would switch around to various kinds of food. And I loved food. And I'd always wanted to break free of those generic fruit loops. The choice of drugs and alcohol changed too—I hadn't always loved drugs and alcohol; didn't even really know too much about them but, hey, two out of three was all that was needed to accept that third element.

All of a sudden, the small town in which I lived had changed for me and was changing me.

One night, during our dancing and drinking, a new person arrived at the house. As I was dancing with a beer in my hand in the living room with my girlfriends, the front door opened, and in walked the boy I'd met a few weeks before at the apartment above the law firm where I had tried drugs for the first time. I remembered his name, Nick. He wore baggy '90s pants and his boxers came above the waistband. His shirt was white with a blue Nike symbol on it. His stocking cap accentuated his face. Even though he was young, he had a slight goatee.

He came in, grabbed a beer, rolled a joint, and sat down on the couch in the living room that was the dance floor. My friend knew that I was giddy inside because when we left the house a few weeks back I had told her that he was cute.

Nick drank his beer and smoked his joint and, as the night went on, he became a little more friendly with people.

Within a couple of hours, he became the DJ, playing hip-hop like Biggie Smalls, Tupac, and Twister. He even danced a little—basically moving his shoulders back and forth; something from a hip-hop music video.

I danced the night past midnight, one, and two—Cinderella did not leave the ball. And, as time went on, Nick and I continued to drink and smoke pot. I let all my inhibitions go. We began flirting with each other. We danced slower and closer. Then, he pulled me in and began to kiss me.

I was excited because he seemed to have the same feelings toward me as I did for him. I became blissfully—though alcohol and drug fueled—over the moon.

On reflection, of course, it looks different. I'm older, wiser, and understand that I wanted to feel physical and emotional attention.

We then found ourselves sneaking up the steep staircase to the bedroom where I'd often crash. I don't think I'd ever flirted before. And I'd never giggled as much. And I'd never done anything like what I'd done or would do.

I was a virgin. I had no clue what I was doing. But he knew what to do. And I let him take the lead.

When we woke, he told me he'd be going home. Back in 1999 there were cellphones. Not smartphones, but cellphones. They were popular, but I did not have one, and I don't think he had one either.

The next weekend came, I headed to the party house early, hoping Nick would be there. I pictured how he'd be as excited to see me as I was to see him.

Nick did show up and we drank Goldschläger. This was a Swiss schnapps flavored with cinnamon. It had actual 24 carat gold flakes in it. It was a big thing to do shots of Goldschläger at that time. Nick and I would get our hands on a bottle of 'gold shocker' and smoke joints between.

We partied for two or three more weekends. Then, he didn't 'show up one weekend and I couldn't figure out why. The next two weeks he was a no-show. I had decided he didn't like me anymore. I even thought he might have a girlfriend. I was pretty much okay with it; it didn't stop my going to the party house.

TAKE AWAYS
ONE

Work on loving yourself so much that you are never tempted to put anyone on a pedestal.

TWO

Never let anyone take your 'first' place.

Experiences on Call

Alfa Bravo Charlie Delta

DISTURBANCE-REPORTED-BY-PARENTS-
PROBLEM-WITH-CHILD-COPY.

Another winter night; cold and miserable but at least it was not snowing. Two parents had reported their son had stolen their car.

I recognized the place from the dispatcher's directions; I'd spoken many times with members of this family, and it wasn't my first time in their home. However, this was the first time for this kind of call.

Normally, I was there for the husband beating up the wife, the wife beating up the husband, parties, drug sells, burglaries, and everything else imaginable, but not a stolen motor vehicle.

The setting comprised a house on a hill, numerous cars scattered along the driveway and through the yard. The property had garbage strewn everywhere. Home appliances created a makeshift fence between the house and the backwoods offering them privacy from the coons and the bears.

This was a 'no one uses their front door around here' kind of place. I approached the back door carefully as every other step was missing. The railing was attached by a single nail, and the door was half open—only a couple of screws holding the hinges to the frame.

I knocked and received a COOOOMMMEEE INNNNNN yelled from the inside of the house. As I slipped inside, roaches scurried from garbage bag to garbage bag, ran up walls, twitched and squeezed through electric sockets, and scuttled behind cupboard doors. I looked to the ceiling—the armored insects were even there, pushing themselves beyond the metal plates around the light fixtures.

Horrified as I was, that wasn't all.

Plunkety, plunk, cockroaches were freefalling from the ceiling onto the kitchen table, counters, and furniture. Everywhere were live and crispy-dead roaches. Everywhere.

"I am here for a report of a stolen vehicle." I was still only in the doorway, forcing myself to maintain my composure, not to dance a jig or a bad tap dance as the roaches continued in motion all around me.

"Come on in out of the cold." The dad slurred his words from behind a haze of cigarette smoke. He was sitting at that same kitchen table that was under attack by the roaches.

I declined politely—told him I'd just stay where I was.

"Right, yes. Sorry about the mess. We need to clean up a little bit," he said.

I braced myself in the door frame as I took notes, all the time praying this was a temperature zone that cockroaches wouldn't dare to cross into. Quickly, but thoroughly, I received all the facts that I needed and exited the home.

Back in the safety of the car, I alerted dispatch that the parents reported their teenage son had taken the car without permission and had been drinking. The son wasn't allowed to take the car, but they had gotten into a fight and the son left intoxicated. He was headed toward the village.

The vehicle's description and that of the boy was relayed over our channel for other officers and deputies, not only in our county but those in surrounding counties.

I headed toward the village to see if I could locate the car. In that village all the government houses looked alike. I drove slowly, looking along all the driveways, through the Native Charter School lots, and around the community center. No luck.

Experience told me that a lot of kids would head out of the county or toward the county line which was just northeast of my location. Though there are a lot of gravel roads that intertwine, they all eventually come back to the village, but a person could easily get lost in the maze in the woods.

I was about a mile and a half from the county road when it started to snow lightly. Between the snow flakes I saw red taillights ahead. I sped up only a little so as not to be perceived as coming up too fast. Three car lengths behind, I identified the license plates as those of the reported car.

912-I'M-RIGHT-BEHIND-THE-VEHICLE-
APPROACHING-COUNTY-LINE-IN-HALF-
A-MILE-REQUEST-BACK-UP-COPY.

I remained behind the vehicle and observed the driving behavior: shoulder line to center line, back to straight, then over to shoulder. At one point, the driver stayed on the shoulder for about a quarter of a mile.

912-INITIATING-TRAFFIC-STOP-COPY.

I flipped the switch for my emergency overhead lights and the driver-boy I was pursuing hit the gas and took off like a bat out of hell.

912-IN-PURSUIT-OF-VEHICLE-LICENSE-
PLATE-XYZ123-NORTHBOUND-
CROSSED-COUNTY-LINE.

Every half mile or so I would give a new location and report the speed and driving behavior. The other county radioed in and provided their locations.

This went on for thirty-miles, until the driver turned the vehicle onto a major state highway; he was headed toward a larger city. The county's deputies reported they were on the highway and about two miles ahead of the pursuit. Others said they were three miles behind. I was relieved I'd got fellow officers in front and behind me.

The ones ahead said they would lay spike strips; hopefully the boy would drive over, the vehicle's tired would be flattened, and he'd pull over.

As we approached the location of where the spike strips were being placed, I could see the emergency lights of the squad cars in front of me and the emergency lights of the other deputies right behind me.

The suspect in the vehicle also knew what was happening and, at about forty-five miles an hour, swerved, went through the median, and began traveling the opposite direction.

I was able to execute a turn and follow—reporting my change of direction to dispatch.

Just as I was calling in a location, a flash of silver and orange streaked from the front seat of the vehicle—I was that close to him.

SHOTS-FIRED-FROM-SUSPECT-
VEHICLE-COPY.

I slowed to put some distance between me and the shooter. The suspect vehicle slowed too. I wasn't even doing twenty-five, and the vehicle I was 'chasing' crept down the right-hand lane. The high-speed pursuit had turned into a turtle race. A few miles later, the vehicle slowly and steadily tracked into the ditch. The deep snow helped it come to a stop.

I lined up with the other officers, a tactical move, behind the vehicle in the ditch. We were still on the highway, blocking all lanes of traffic. I yelled as loud as I could, duty weapon engaged on the driver's side. Over and over and over I shouted, 'COME OUT WITH YOUR HANDS UP.' But there was no movement.

I slowly approached the driver's side door, being careful it wasn't an ambush—I didn't want to be a victim to someone who was just going to jump out and start shooting.

Officers from other agencies approached the other side of the car. One of my colleagues shouted that the driver was shot.

I grabbed the door handle and opened the car door.

It was a horrible sight: where one of his eyes should have been there was a gaping hole; blood was gushing from that space.

He was still seat-belted, and he was alive.

We were able to cut the seatbelt and get the boy out onto the pavement and render first aid until the ambulance arrived and transported the suspect to the hospital.

Paperwork followed, and I was done.

About nine months later, I was patrolling on an evening shift, and stopped at a gas station to grab some snacks and use their restroom. As I was standing at the counter waiting to pay for my merchandise, the guy in front of me paid, then turned and gazed at me. Immediately, I saw that one eye was glazed over and gray—like cremated ashes, lifeless, soulless. The other eye was walnut and moon-shaped, though there was no emotion displayed from that one either.

I was frozen in time by his eyes, and he held that gaze. Then I realized the young man in front of me was the suspect from the chase nine-months earlier.

He was alive. I was relieved. His heart was pumping blood. He had a glass eye. I wondered how he now viewed the world. I gave thanks for all the people who had contributed to saving his life. And I held compassion for the situation he had grown up in, and for his parents and the situation they'd likely been raised in. Then I checked in with compassion and its cousin, forgiveness, and sprinkled a little of that around in myself and toward others in my life at that time.

Echo Foxtrot Golf Hotel

NUMEROUS-REPORTS-HEAD-ON-
COLLISION-INVOLVING-A-SEMI-ROUTE-
42-FIVE-MILES- SOUTH-OF-CITY-
LIMITS-COPY.

The heaviness of greasy fries, mozzarella sticks, and pizza lingered in the air. Diesel fumes traveled inside, hanging on the clothes of customers. Wet floors were slippery from the snow that had been falling for ages from the black night sky.

I sat in a single booth next to the chip isle of the local gas station, eating my sandwich, facing the door. Outside, the flashing lights of the casino flickered and highlighted the houses and yards along the highway which held its own black glare.

Soon, bars would close, and people would try to outsmart the police by choosing 'the right route home'.

I'd said 'hi' to a few locals and regulars who were getting fueled up before the night rush. While having an argument in my head about whether I should or shouldn't get a bag of chips, a female I knew well because I'd arrested her a few times, and been to her residence for many calls, walked in and grabbed some food from the grease box located next to the counter. I decided to get the bag of chips and get in line behind the female I knew.

She turned and looked at me. She seemed more responsible than I remembered. Dressed in black slacks, blue and black uniform top, and a name badge around her neck, like a neck-lace—yes, you notice these things—she said, "Hi, how are you doing?"

"Good, how are you?" I answered and asked.

"Good," she said. "Just off work and on my way to pick up my kids. Have a good night and drive safe." She paid for her food and walked back to a silver car parked at the pumps.

I watched her get in. The back end of the vehicle was almost touching the ground—as if there were no shocks in it.

Back in the booth, next to the chip aisle, I started to crunch on mine and flipped to the auto newspaper on the table's top. Five minutes later—I n full stuff-the-chips-down mode, because cops eat fast as do most first responders; if you don't eat now, you never know when your next meal will be—my radio went off.

DISPATCH-TO-912-COPY

"912. Go ahead," I said.

WE-HAVE-NUMEROUS-REPORTS-OF-
A-HEAD-ON-COLLISION-SEMI-VERSUS-
CAR-ABOUT-FIVE-MILES-SOUTH-OF-
CITY-COPY

"Ten-four. En route," I said.

In crisis mode I grab the mostly empty bag of chips and my diet Coke and head for the door. Chips and soda in my duty bag on the passenger side, I take off. Skillfully and responsibly, I make my way through the ice and snow on the unplowed highway in the direction of the accident.

As I pull up, I see a semi truck and trailer that was originally traveling north now three-quarters of the way blocking the southbound lane—it's entire cab in the ditch. I can't see a second vehicle. I stop a long way back, way too long, thinking that I would stop to block traffic far enough back because the highway was not lit.

As I called in my location and requested backup for traffic management on a state highway, a teenage boy I knew from when I was a school resource officer (SRO) came running up to my vehicle, waving his hands and frantically screaming, "There's a head lying in the road. Over there."

He indicated about 25 feet away. I asked him to stay in his car where he was warm and began walking in the indicated direction.

Though I did not see the head, I saw an arm, and a partial leg in the road. Then I noticed the vehicle a few yards in front of me—a silver one. All I could tell was the color because it was crushed to the size of, well, it might have been a matchbox. The front end of the vehicle was pushed all the way through the back seat as if the front seat never existed.

My partner came from the other direction. I proceeded toward the semi when I noticed the face of a female on the ground. Yes, the face, not the whole head. It was as if someone had meticulously taken a scalpel and precisely carved the skin about 1 inch thick from the chin all the way around the hair line, and back down the other side, forming and leaving the perfect mask on the frozen pavement of the road.

I was shaken. I'd never seen this before in real life. It looked like a mask from Halloween. But I knew it was not.

I then proceeded to walk toward the semi truck and, as I rounded the front to get to the driver's side, I noticed the grill.

Four full fingers, all with rings on them, stuck to the metal, as if it was a grotesque hood ornament.

I was further shaken but, at these times, a person doesn't have time to process that trauma; they just have to say WTF and keep doing the job. This is how police and other first responders are wired.

I climbed up the cab of the semi truck and looked inside. There sat a man with glazed eyes. He stared straight forward. Was not moving. I knocked on the window to see if he could open the door, but there was no response. I pulled the handle and the door popped open. The driver of the semi turned his head and looked at me in complete shock. I asked him if he was okay—in terms of physical injury. He told me he thought he was. He looked himself over and I looked him over and he decided he needed to get out. He exited the semi and immediately got on his cellphone with the company he was driving for. Then returned to the front seat of his truck.

I stayed on the scene until the ambulance arrived to check out the semi driver, and until state patrol arrived to map out the crash scene—those officers carefully map out the scene as county deputies stand shivering in the below freezing temperatures. For a few hours the highway was closed as state patrol investigated the scene.

By this time, the body parts were frozen to the highway.

As the semi was pulled out of the ditch, and the silver car was placed onto a flat bed to be towed, we were given the okay to continue our work. It took a shovel to scrape the body parts off the ground, after which those parts of a human were sent with state patrol for further investigation.

No, she didn't get to pick up her children.

Bad things happen to good people.

It's not fair that bad things happen to people who have broken the cycle.

I hated that this happened to her.

I hated it so much that I had to try to forget it so that the unfairness didn't eat me alive.

I saw unfairness every day.

Let's Coach

Teresa: My childhood wasn't that great, but I tell myself others had it worse and not to get all upset about mine. But I'm stuck. I can't help feeling some frustration with the past, and that it is holding me back. How do I navigate the journey of looking back at the choppy waters of the past?

Let's get one thing on the table: we are not on this earth to compare ourselves to others—not their happy times or their sad times. What is true for you is true for you, and that is what counts.

When I first started working in the police force and saw people who had less than I had, I'd think that my troubles—past or present—were less valid than theirs. I'd constantly tell myself to suck it up. Well, sucking it up really means pushing it down. Down so far that it becomes difficult to deal with. Every 'body', mind, and soul belongs, and is equal in deserving empathy, understanding, and kindness. Please remember to give to yourself first, and to hold space for yourself first—embrace self compassion and validate your memories without rating them.

Everyone is unique, and there are many ways to view and then learn from the past. What I think I hear you asking is 'how does someone start?' I say that because it is a journey with many diversions and some backtracking. Start by grabbing a pen and paper and write down where you want to be (not where you've been). Certainly, think about your past, but focus on where you would like to be when you think of the present or the future. Write where do you see yourself when you feel like you aren't being held back anymore? How do you feel about your past? What are your frustrations? Why is it frustrating to you? Start by peeling the onion layer by layer. Go deep within yourself.

What do you feel is holding you back, exactly? Start there. Write down your exact feelings. Who was there, where do you feel those feeling are at in your body? Tell yourself exactly where you feel stuck. This is where you start. If you don't start somewhere, you won't make it through it.

Let's Coach

Hey, Teresa... I believe you when you say it is good to be childlike, but how do I engage with that childlike me that used to enjoy the kinds of things you've mentioned in 'your golden place'—those 'fireflies in a jar kinds of moments'—when it seems to me the only people who can do that kind of thing are wealthy and have lots of free time? Face it, I'd look stupid running through a field with a glass jar—someone would call the police for sure.

Stop. Close your eyes after you read this next sentence:

Whose voice is it in your head that is telling you that you'd look stupid?

Okay, whose was it?

For many of us it will be a parent's voice, or a strict teacher—like a voice that you've created from all the critics in your past who told you certain things were a waste of time.

Let's step back now and look at ourselves in a mirror—real or imaginary as you read these words. Are you not the same body, albeit larger, as you were when you were a child? Are those the same eyes that you looked at the world with when you were six, nine, and thirteen?

The child we were not only lives within us but is us. We have just matured in years and collected a lot of information over those years.

Hand on heart. That's the heart that was beating when you came into the world. Now, hold your own hand. That's the same hand you had when you were a little one.

You infer you've had some childlike fun before. Here's what I think would be amazing: pick the one or two things that you loved doing and do it. It could be as simple as folding a piece of paper into a fortune teller, or sitting on a wall high enough that your feet don't touch the ground so you can swing them. It might be wearing bright yellow—or a color you don't wear now. Maybe you had a stuffie you slept with—go get one. Is there an ice cream parlor nearby, or something similar? Can you take your little-child-self there and just let her order what she wants? Bubble gum, tiger-tiger, a banana split, a hot fudge sundae? When was the last time you walked through a toy department in a store. Get that ninja turtle or Hot Wheels. Plan to dress up this Halloween, even if you're not going anywhere but the door.

If someone has never had those childhood events and craves them, the same advice is valid.

Take some sheets and hang them over the table or some other point in your house or apartment and make a tent, and sleep in it—watch The Secret Garden or another childhood favorite when you're in there.

Let's Coach

I know I have toxic family members and friends, but I feel obligated to them. How do I stop this?

You are either the passenger or the driver in your own life. When it comes to negative, toxic energy you have a responsibility to protect yourself... but I recognize we're not all trained to understand our responsibilities since we may have been socialized around toxicity. The answer is to invest in yourself.

First, I would suggest thinking about your boundaries around your energy. Deep down, how do you want to feel when you are around others? And do you feel that way when it comes to the people you've referred to in your question?

The second thing is to decide how much contact you want—in other words: defining your boundaries. Do you want to break free from them altogether? Do you want to still be friends with them and/or be able to be around them at certain gatherings that have meaning to you?

To help you figure out where they will fit in your new life—where you will accept them and what you will accept—try this:

Write down what makes them toxic and what you would want to change when around them.

Now, knowing you can't change them, but you can change what you accept, set a timeline and a set of guidelines around how long you would be willing to be around them, and what events you are willing to be at when they are in attendance. Sometimes it might be the place—for example, maybe their behavior is more acceptable at a coffee shop than in a bar.

When you are at events with them, or in their company, be ready to divert the conversation away from toxic talk. Engage in a positive redirection.

If this does not work, go to your plan B which you have previously decided upon. That could be excusing yourself, or it could be being direct and explaining when 'this comes up' or 'that comes up' you cannot and will not engage. That way they have the opportunity to respond. Prepare for a reaction—defensiveness, standing their ground, even name calling you (or saying you're too serious, a snob, or out of line). Make sure you are ready to respond to those without getting into a toxic battle. Leaving doesn't mean storming out, but it still means leaving.

Remember, you need to protect your energy and when you chose to change the path you are on you need to be aware you might lose friends or family in the process.

The more you practice positive engagement, and setting boundaries, the more new friends you will find who have similar values. Sometimes, your example will bring family members or current toxic friends around to their own changes—but that is not your frontline job.

Show your friends and family what really matters to you and that you want to focus on the positive things that are happening in your life. Most of all let them know where you want to invest your energy and time and invite them along. In many cases, actions speak louder than words. And, with boundary setting, it's about taking action to take care of yourself.

Part Two: Resilience

Recap

…I'd gone from never using drugs, to going with a friend to an apartment above a business in a converted house, to meeting Nick, to using pot and partying every weekend at a house where the living room was a dance floor. Nick had showed up there and we'd become close. Someone cared about me—dare I say, loved me? I had no idea how babies were made—none. We drank Goldschläger. We were intimate in the bedroom I used and that was reached by almost unclimbable stairs. For weeks after, we continued to see each other on weekends at the party house. And then he stopped coming…

The Bathroom

It was January 1999; I had been sixteen years old for less than three months. About six weeks had gone by since Nick and I'd first danced the night away and then slept upstairs in the bedroom I used at the party house.

One day, midweek, Crystal and I decided to head to the party house to check on the plans for the upcoming weekend. While we were there, I went into the tiny bathroom. I recall that the door was cracked open a bit so I could still talk to Crystal about who we'd invite and what fun we'd have on the weekend.

As I was sitting on the toilet, something came to my mind. I couldn't remember when I'd had my last period. Had it been before Christmas? Had it been since Halloween?

The next thing I realized was that I had no one in my family to talk to.

I washed my hands, left the bathroom, looked at Crystal, and told her that I hadn't had my period in a while.

"Oh my God," she said. "Are you pregnant?"

I stood there in the kitchen of the party house, feeling really dumb, and said, "Crystal, I don't know how a person gets pregnant."

The ridiculousness of this question hit me then, and still hits me now. I'd grown up in a house of six siblings and me.

My siblings had children, I was regularly drinking alcohol and doing drugs, and I had no idea how someone became pregnant.

In Little Blue, certain subjects were taboo. Mom and Dad never showed any affection for each other—I never saw them kiss or hug or heard them tell each other 'I love you'.

My friend, Crystal, was a couple of years older than me. She knew all about intimacy, sexual conduct, sexual intercourse, sexual arousal, and sexual anything. She was the one friend who helped me understand what had happened. She explained a whole bunch of things, then asked if I'd had sex with anybody.

I laughed awkwardly and said that now that I knew what it was, yes, I'd had sex with Nick at that first party.

Crystal asked if he'd worn a condom.

I told her that it had been my first time ever having sex, didn't know it was sex until she'd explained it just now, and I had no idea if he wore a condom.

"Girl, I think you're pregnant," she said.

At that moment, my chest became tight, and my breathing got faster. It was a fight or flight moment. My body felt warm, and my insides seemed to be fuzzy—all the physical symptoms of an anxiety attack.

Questions sped like remote controlled race cars on a track in my head. They went faster and faster until I could not separate one question or thought from another. How could I be pregnant? What would I tell Mom and Dad? What would I do? How can this be?

My brain decided that the best way to deal with not breaking down was just to say, 'let's give it a few days; maybe my period is a little bit late. After all, there's been a lot of drugs and alcohol consumption, so maybe the system is a little off.'

And that is what I did. I waited a few days. Bought myself some time to calm and not think that pregnancy was close to being true.

Clinic

The following week, Crystal and I met again at the party house during the day. She asked me if my period had started.

I told her it hadn't and that I had nobody to talk to. I asked her what I should do.

Crystal said that she would take me to a place where we could get a pregnancy test.

We jumped into her little station wagon and headed across town, all the way up the strip, past the beach, past the water slide, past the gas stations, the dental offices, and past the little brown building that we called the mall. We crossed over the road and headed into a more desolate area of the city and pulled into a dark gray-black building.

Crystal went inside with me and, as we approached the front desk, she said to the woman at reception, "My friend needs a pregnancy test."

The woman at the front desk looked at me and asked Crystal how old I was. Crystal answered for me: sixteen.

The front desk lady handed me a clipboard with some papers attached to it. She asked me to fill out the forms and bring them back when I was finished.

My hand shook as I held the pen and read the questions. Was I under eighteen-years-old? The next question was: 'if YES, print names of parents.'

I did not print their names.

With Crystal's guidance, I made it through all the paperwork and returned it to the lady. She told me to have a seat, someone would be with me shortly.

My nervousness, fear, and a thousand more emotions kept me silent. Crystal said nothing either. During our silent, sitting-on-chairs time, a nurse came into the reception area and began reading the paperwork. From there I was taken into a little room and the nurse began reading the same questions to me that I had just written the answers to. I had to answer each one aloud. I was two inches tall, filled with shame as I answered. Even though Crystal was there, I have never felt so lonely in my life.

When the questioning was over, the nurse handed me a cup and asked me to go into the bathroom and provide a sample. I left the cup of pee in the bathroom as I'd been asked, then went back to reception where I was told they'd be with me shortly.

All through the waiting, I kept thinking how my life was over. How would I finish school? What would Mom say? What would Dad say? What would my friends think of me?

Then it hit me. Should I go and tell Nick?

Every minute that passed in the tiny room in the gray and black clinic felt like an hour. Every second of every minute that felt like an hour in which I prayed that I was not pregnant.

There was a knock on the door.

"I have your results," said the nurse.

And then the earth shifted.

"You are pregnant," she said.

It knocked the wind out of my lungs. I couldn't breathe. I was hyperventilating. Then I began to cry. A lot. I recall the nurse looking at Crystal. The expression on her face was a mixture of 'I don't know what to say to her' and 'I don't know what to do to make this easier for her'.

It was Crystal who responded. She hugged me, then helped me pull myself together. She said we'd get through this, and she'd help me figure out what to do.

I remember leaving the clinic and getting into the little station wagon as if it were a moment ago, but I don't recall where we drove to, how long it took, and what happened the rest of that day.

My heart messaged me: I will not be Shelly,

I remained silent for a few days. Crystal and I met at the party house and discussed how to tell my Mom and Dad, went over what they might do, and then got into the heavy discussion of if I should tell Nick.

The decision was that I would. The following weekend, I went to the party house hoping that I would run into Nick, and then somehow magically come up with the words to let him know that I was pregnant with his child. But Nick never showed up that Friday night just as he hadn't the past few Friday nights.

I began to wonder how I could get hold of him to tell him the news. I kept coming back to the only way I could find him was to return to the two-storey house, climb the back staircase, and knock on that apartment door.

My mind was flooded with questions: Did he have a girlfriend? What if I went over there and there was another girl with him? What would he say when I told him I was pregnant? As I went over these questions it was clear to me that I was filled with fear. I was not planning to say anything other than I was pregnant. I certainly wasn't planning to say that we had to be together from that moment on. I wasn't expecting him to say we'd raise the child. I just felt he had the right to know.

The following weekend I mustered up the strength and courage to go to the apartment to tell him. I asked Becky for a ride back to the white, two-storey that sat behind the brown brick mall.

We pulled into the alleyway and followed all the rules we had before—slow down, lower the music, shut off the headlights. We parked behind the stairs. I sat in the car for ages, working up the courage get out of the vehicle and go up the stairs to see if Nick was home.

I questioned myself: Why am I doing this? Do I really need to tell him? What if he isn't even home? Will they open the door for me?

I opened and closed the car's door ever-so-quietly. Immediately, I felt the chill of winter. There was ice and snow on the ground. I grabbed onto the freezing cold railing and began the climb, one step at a time, really slowly.

Halfway up the stairs, from behind, I was violently and aggressively thrown onto the stairs and landed on my stomach. I had no clue who had attacked me or why.

The next thing I knew was that I had been handcuffed, brought down the stairs, and put into a squad car.

I sat in the squad car for a while, not being able to see what was going on outside because the windows were fogged up.

Then, the officer I knew—Officer E—got into the car. "Are you buying drugs, Teresa?" he asked. "Do you have anything on you?

I was terrified; had no idea what was happening around me. I'd only ever seen a drug bust on television shows. I told Officer E I was there to speak with a guy named Nick because I had to tell him something. He didn't believe me. Eventually, I broke down crying. I sobbed out that I wasn't there to buy drugs. I didn't even know if anyone was going to be home. I confessed that I had come to the house to tell Nick that I was pregnant with his child.

At this point, Officer E uncuffed me and told me to go home.

The car I'd arrived in was gone. I walked across town in the freezing cold winter night all the way back to Becky's house. As I approached the house, I saw her car parked outside and the lights in the house were on. I went in the front door and couldn't believe it—she was there.

She told me that as she was waiting for me, squad cars pulled into the area, so she'd headed home.

I then told her the story that I knew about me walking up the stairs and how I was tackled, placed in handcuffs, and questioned. Neither one of us could believe that this happened.

We waited for about an hour or so, then we drove back to the white, two-storey house. First, we went by the mall to see the house from a distance. The squad cars were still there; there appeared to be lots of commotion in the alley. We drove until the cops were gone and then drove into the alley like any normal person would. This time I wasn't nervous about telling Nick that I was pregnant because that fear was trumped by my concern of the police coming back, and what trouble Nick might be in.

When I arrived at the little platform outside of the door, I knocked. No one answered. There was no music coming from the place like there had been on the first visit. I knocked again and I heard someone walking toward the door. "It's Teresa," I called out and knocked again. "Let me in."

Nick cracked open the door. When he finally opened it all the way, I walked to the tiny kitchen with the round table. I was not nervous. We had a short conversation and then the words just came out and, before I knew it, I'd told him I was pregnant.

Shock registered on Nick's face. Several minutes of complete silence passed—except for the music coming out of his room.

He didn't throw me out. He took it all in. He was only seventeen—not yet an adult. He had a vehicle that was stored, because it was a low-rider used for fun in the summer. Neither of us were prepared for regular life as an adult, let alone with a child. I remember saying to him that I didn't know what I was going to do. Nick agreed that he didn't either.

With the announcement off my chest, I knew the next thing that I had to do was to tell Mom and Dad.

I would be a parent. I would not be Shelly. I would do what I had to do to raise my child. I would work. I would pick her up at her caregiver after work. I would do everything in my power to be a responsible, hardworking mom. I'd have a car—sure it'd be old—and I'd work shiftwork, even if that meant nightwork in crappy jobs, I'd do it and then I'd leave work and come home to my child.

Rooms in a Green House

I chose a time when I knew Mom and Dad would be home; borrowed a friend's car and drove across town. No, I didn't have a driver's license. It had been hard to get used to not going all the way up the hill to Little Blue. I parked on the street in front of the green house where we'd moved to; a place where I had been spending less and less time.

The green house had a large picture window, but I'd never sat in a rocking chair looking out at the world. I'd been outside in another world. I walked down the driveway, around the back of the house, and up onto the deck.

The back door led straight into the kitchen in which there was an island. The hub was a dining area beyond the kitchen. Mom and Dad had a round table surrounded by captain's chairs with padded, cloth arms.

Mom was sitting at the table, smoking a cigarette. I could see right through to the living room, and past its big window to where the car I'd borrowed was parked. To the side of the living room was a set of stairs leading up to the second floor where there were three bedrooms and a bathroom.

"I have something I need to tell you," I said.

Just as I spoke, Dad came down the stairs, through the living room and into the dining area.

Anxiety kicked in and I began to sweat. I was afraid they would flash back to Shelly and think I was sleeping around when, in reality, I had not been.

The words, 'I am pregnant' came out mumbled.

Mom said virtually nothing. Not really any questions. Dad flew into a rage. He yelled at me to the point that I became scared. He told me they were not about to raise another baby. Then he told me to get out.

Hyena

I have it in me so much nearer home
To scare myself with my own desert places.
—Robert Frost

When she returned to Detroit Lakes, even though she'd been in crisis, her needs were still not met, and so she began to find people who could be 'her home'. Back in Minnesota, there was no welcoming committee. There was no 'we're so glad you're back, thank heaven you're safe.' I'm sure they were happy she was home and safe, but it wasn't expressed. My heart began to ache for them, for everyone in the family—clearly my compassion course had paid off. Still, Teresa was my human, and I remained completely loyal to her.

But I wasn't enough for Teresa. It wasn't like she knew that I was there, and we just hung out like a cool-looking-radical-dog (hyenas are not dogs) and a girl.

Teresa found others who were also searching for more than they had. They hung out together. I trailed behind, and sometimes raced ahead to remove barriers. But I couldn't always keep up. Thank goodness for the trust she'd put in Officer E. Sometimes I was grateful to be a guide and not a human parent on earth—I don't think I could survive the worry. My Teresa was impulsive and strong. When she was in that river, all I could think about was hypothermia. That, and how would Carol and Gary feel if they knew she was so at risk that she could die. She was physically in the current of a river in the winter.

It was all I could do to hang on to the other end of the branch that Teresa caught so that it wouldn't break away from its trunk. Not only that, but her friend was also in the river, and I had to trust that the friend had a guide as well.

It didn't end there. When the police threatened her with the dog, I wondered if that dog would sense me. Well, of course it would. Dogs are much more evolved than humans. I wondered if I could communicate with it in a different way than I did with humans. Then I discovered I could. It still didn't keep Teresa safe from humans, only from dogs.

If the river wasn't enough of a scare, then her next moves were even more dangerous. She was searching. Searching hard. She was hurting. Even though I could be in the house with her, walk right into the house and sit right beside her, it wasn't enough. Even though I slept at the bottom of the bed and curled up in the vee of her bent legs, behind her knees, that closeness did nothing but help her sleep better. She still became more determined to find her way with new friends.

It seemed she'd hardly dried off from the river than she was heading up a fire escape at the pretty white house that was a law firm downstairs and an apartment upstairs. And how ironic was that? Law below, drugs above.

I tugged on the bottom of her jeans all the way up, but she was strong, determined, and focused on finding new. I slipped in behind her at the apartment and, smoky as it was, I could see, after her initial fear, that she saw something that wasn't in Little Blue. There was a taste of what was at Tammy's home that I always thought of was 'the Golden place'. There was a group of people who were wanting to be together and were laughing and being silly with each other, sharing stories, and 'not working'. It was a different kind of safe. Risky, yes, in terms of the drug. But there was a genuine feeling of being there for each other. Teresa wanted that more than she wanted to see that this could lead to what Shelly had gotten herself into.

I understood it. And I understood Shelly a little more in that moment as well.

The party house was similar. A place to be herself, to do the thing she loved—dancing. But there was a price to pay, and she couldn't see it.

I made some advance plans again, to keep her safe through her treacherous journey ahead. It would still be difficult, and there would be a setback or two or ten, but it would be worth it because another beautiful human would come out of it all. And that would shift Teresa's views. But there was so much to go through with her. I dodged her crazy steps when she was dancing, I squeezed myself into that tiny bathroom when she realized what was probably happening, and I held her up when Carol and Gary reacted hostilely to her news. I threw myself under her when she was pulled and dropped from the fire escape so that her head wouldn't hit the ground. But I never left her side and I never questioned why I was with her. That is the job of a guide. Even a novice one.

It would come to be that she would have to make a home, since she could not find one where she belonged.

And she did that by creating a home for her baby in utero, then through Nick's original buy-in and him taking her seriously, and through his mother's actions, and a whole group of humans whose compassion came together to join with Teresa's determination and hard work.

There was universal support with a twist because there were still many lessons to be learned.

The most amazing thing about my Teresa, though, was that after she'd learned she was pregnant, she stood in front of the mirror, looked into her own eyes and said, "I will not be Shelly."

I sat proudly beside her, my head looking up at her beautiful strength. I knew in that moment that, while there would still be tough times ahead, she was saying the strongest thing she could at that moment. I knew that one day she would know it meant: "I will be me. Uniquely me. I will be successful. I will be unmesswithable."

I knew that she would understand that being Shelly didn't make Shelly a terrible person, but one to hold compassion for in that Shelly had her own story. But at that moment, I knew it was a driving force. And I supported it because it was her way out. To state what she would not be.

I would have many more proud moments, as a guide for Teresa, but this one shifted not only the earth under my ethereal paws, but the heavens as well.

Basement

I had only, within days, had the official word. I was pregnant.

Where was I going to live? How would I get food? What would I do? I returned to Nick's apartment and told him how badly it went down with Mom and Dad. He'd told his parents already, and his dad allowed me to stay in the apartment. Nick and I did some talking and realized living with his dad was not a solution.

Then Nick's mom showed up. She said that we should go and stay with her, and she would help support us through the pregnancy, and help us raise the child.

Even though I had not met her before, she grabbed me, hugged me, and told me I was beautiful. I felt supported and I trusted her. I felt so welcomed. We made plans to move to her house within the week, Nick packed up his belongings, and I was able to return 'home' where Mom and Dad allowed me to take some of my belongings from their house.

Nick's mom's place was a forty-five-minute drive from Detroit Lakes.

We drove for what seemed forever through winding roads lined with tall trees. Thick forests surrounded us, the occasional lake appearing in the distance. A large brown house sat at the end of a treed driveway.

I was overwhelmed in a good way.

Inside the house, I took in the large living room with a sliding door to a patio which overlooked a lake. It was beautiful.

Stairs led to a basement which Nick's mom said she envisioned as a living space for us. Though it wasn't fancy, like upstairs, and it was concrete floored with rugs overtop, it was a place for the two of us to lay our heads. We were so thankful. Her love and support were incredible.

Nick's mom bought me a book about having a baby: *What to Expected When You Are Expecting*. Many nights, Nick and I lay beside each other reading this book and discussing some of the topics in the book. His mom also helped me get in with the primary care provider for a check-up, and a doctor who would follow me through my entire pregnancy. Being that I was so young, and having been a premature baby myself, I visited the doctor more often than most women. Nick came to every appointment. He held my hand and listened to what the doctor said. He was excited, I was scared. We were still kids. Neither one of us had our own vehicle, and we were living far from where we could get regular jobs. With both of us under eighteen, we couldn't get our own apartment either.

During the next couple of months, Dad calmed somewhat, and Nick and I borrowed his mom's car and visited. During this time, Mom and Dad had sold the green house and moved to another part of town to a new one-storey house—I think the stairs had become difficult for Mom, and they were looking for what might be their final 'retirement' home.

During my first trimester, at one of those visits to their new house, Dad suggested he speak to a lawyer and see if I could be granted emancipation. That would mean Mom and Dad would give up their legal rights to me and I'd be able to act as my own person, as if I was eighteen. We knew that by the time the baby was born, Nick would be eighteen, but I'd only be seventeen.

When we returned to Nick's mom's that evening, and shared Dad's idea, she said she wanted us to stay with her. She also supported her son's need to provide for his new family. Happy as we were in Nick's mom's beautiful home, Nick wanted to get a job and start saving for our family. He wanted to do the right thing and get a job and a place in the city.

Those were the days that jobs and homes were advertised in the newspaper, not online. That night we opened the pages to see what was available in Detroit Lakes. We sat in the basement on the bed with that newspaper open and a pen in hand and started looking at different apartments for rent. We looked for places that were close enough to places we might be able to work, so we could walk to work.

We circled a few jobs that we were interested in. We found a few places we could ask about renting. The next morning, we woke up excited to start calling people for potential jobs and rentals. Though we had no success in any of our calls, we didn't give up. We continued the routine.

A couple weeks later, Dad called to let me know that he'd spoken with an attorney and the emancipation could take place since I was pregnant and no longer living at home.

Mom and Dad were sitting at the table when we arrived. Dad handed me a single page document from the attorney. The paper scared me, even though I knew it offered freedom. I'd be making adult decisions on my own at sixteen. That was terrifying.

The positive was that Mom and Dad seemed to understand Nick and I were taking the situation seriously. They knew we were looking for jobs. Dad said that when we found a place, he'd help Nick get a job at the grocery store where Dad worked as a baker. Nick graciously accepted that offer. For the first time, I knew Dad cared and wanted us to succeed.

We returned to Nick's mom's and continued to look for apartments. The problem was, when we called, no one knew what emancipation was. That's when Nick's mom said perhaps we should go to the social services department and ask them if they could help us find a place. We did that the next day.

We explained that we were under the age of eighteen and were expecting a child. The staff there said that they'd seen similar situations many times, but not necessarily from someone so young. They were so respectful that I didn't feel judged. They said they would do much more than find us a home; they'd provide extra help until we were on our feet and working at full-time jobs. They started us on a form of support that included food stamps and medical insurance. They also gave us a number for the local housing.

We filled out all the paperwork for everything with guidance from one of the workers. We received brochures and pamphlets that explained each form of aid, and we were able to obtain vouchers for foods that were considered necessary for a pregnant woman, The office provided prenatal vitamins and explained why it was important I took them.

We drove over to the housing department. There was an old man working the front desk. We explained why we were there, and we showed him all our paperwork. He explained that there'd be an apartment available before the baby was born, but he didn't have one now. He gave us more forms to fill out and asked us for a deposit of $300.00.

Neither of us had the money, but we told him, if he'd put our file on hold, we'd come back next week—we'd find a way to earn that money.

We were excited that we'd have a place and couldn't wait to tell both sets of parents.

On our arrival 'home', we explained to Nick's mom we'd only need to stay a couple more months. She began talking about the furniture we could take from her house.

Nick spoke to her about earning $300.00. Could he do some yard work? Were there things she would have paid others to do? Nick's mom began phoning people; before the end of the night, she had jobs lined up for him at his uncle's, his grand-parents', and her own place. The next day, Nick followed his mom's lead, and spoke to other family who lived along the same road. He added to the jobs that had to be done. Shortly after, Nick was cutting down trees, shoveling, getting houses cleaned up for spring. He worked so hard he made well over $300.00. He made enough to pay our first month's rent and the deposit. I was proud of him, and he was proud of himself.

The belief in us and the support we received—without any judgment—changed the attitude of two teenage party-goers. The following week we drove back into town with his mom's car, pulled into the Housing Authority's parking lot, and proudly walked inside with a money order for the deposit and the first month's rent. The old guy at the desk smiled a huge smile. He seemed as happy about the apartment as we were.

Then he recorded the payment and said, "I have great news for you. Your apartment will be available sooner than expected." He jotted down the address.

We left the building as fast as we could. As we drove to the address to check out where we'd be living, I noticed that we were driving in the direction of Mom and Dad's new place.

As we approached the neighborhood, I thought we'd be turning into an apartment building, but no... the address we'd been given matched to a row of eight townhomes in a little development. We'd imagined being on a walk up where we'd be dragging a car seat and stroller. This was fantastic. It was a two-bedroom townhouse on three levels. Behind the townhomes was a small park. Since the house was vacant and going to be worked on, a manager there offered to take us through.

The living room was large, and the kitchen was perfect, and there was a dining room. Upstairs was a large main bedroom and a smaller bedroom for our baby. Between the two rooms was a bathroom. The unit had a basement where the washer and dryer would be. We talked about how this was perfect for us. Our baby would grow, and we'd be able to go to the park behind. It was central enough for both of us to go to work.

Dark Room

After we stood in the place that would be ours, we drove half a block to Mom and Dad's. I told Mom that I needed to show her something; I asked her to look through her back window. "See those brown townhouses right there? Well, that's where Nick and I will be living in a few weeks."

Though Mom seemed to be happy, she didn't show much emotion. Dad's response was, 'no shit'. We chatted a bit and then Dad said to Nick that he'd like him to go and apply at the grocery store, and to let him know when that was done so Dad could get him hired.

The moment Dad said that, Nick stood and headed out of the house—he didn't want to waste any time. Off he went to the grocery store.

While Nick was gone, Darcie showed up.

I found myself in an unusual situation; Mom and Darcie engaged me in conversation at the table. They were asking what I was going to do about school? What would I do about a job? How did I plan for school and work while raising a child?

"I'm not wasting my time," I said. "I'm taking courses to get my GED and make something of myself." Suddenly, anxiety and nervousness overwhelmed me. I wasn't good enough for them. I wasn't good enough. I didn't know how to answer all the questions. I explained to them that Nick and I knew we needed to work, and we'd work hard to keep our place.

At that point, I knew that I could not know it all. We were just taking things day by day and navigating the unknown. What I also knew was that navigating it with support was a whole lot better than talk that intimidated or was negative. Was I worried and scared? Hell, yeah!

I sat facing two women—my Mom, who was my biological grandmother, and my sister, who was really my biological aunt, the curse-of-Shelly hanging over my head, Mom and Darcie started in on options.

"You don't have to have this baby," said Darcie.

"What do you mean?" I asked.

"You could carry this baby and give it up for adoption," she replied. Mom nodded in agreement.

My face began to burn. Anger and sadness replaced the joy and promise I'd brought into the house. I was four months at least. Nick and I had come together and overcome challenges that were far more complex than any teens usually faced. We'd seen ourselves as a family. Why destroy that vision? Or ignore the work we'd done?

There was an expression on Darcie's face, her body shifted, and her eyes traveled to Mom, and avoided me.

"You could abort the baby." She stayed fixed on Mom. "But you would have to do it soon."

Confusion, shock, and utter disgust filled my mind and showed on my face. They both sat there staring at me. Mom became less engaged, and her attention drifted to the television which was tuned to a soap opera. I knew this was her coping mechanism; her style was to be a part of conversations, but not speak in them. Mom looked at me occasionally, but Darcie was determined to get an answer.

"You're asking me to get an abortion?" I asked.

"It is one of the options I am letting you know about." She put her hands up to her shoulders and then shrugged.

In that moment, I was alone, the little girl growing up without anyone seeing or hearing her.

With Mom's lack of engagement, but seemingly a buy-in, and Darcie's approach, I became physically cold; an abandoned child. I was desperate for a warm embrace, for a strong person to stand next to me and say, everything will be fine. I wanted to hear: this may not be easy, but you are a strong, capable individual. I wanted badly for someone to say something like, your dreams can still come true, maybe not as quickly as you had planned, but you will make it happen. Instead, I was being told that I was not capable, that I could not do it, that I would be nothing in life if I had the baby... my baby.

Those exact words may not have come out of their mouths, but that is what I heard.

Click, click, click, click was the only sound I could hear in the room. The walls were closing in. Click, click, click, click as the seconds ticked away on the old clock hanging on the wall. Seconds seemed like hours. How much longer until Nick was done and would be back to rescue me from the horror movie I was in?

The drive home offered the silent calm of the car. Adoption? Abortion? I played various scenarios in my head on the long drive back to Nick's mom's house. Picturing the months ahead with a baby tumbling inside me, and then, on the day of the child's birth, saying goodbye. Handing the baby to people I knew nothing about because my own family didn't believe Nick and I could be parents.

I pictured myself walking through picketers holding signs and shouting "murderer" as I walked into a nondescript building. I saw myself in a waiting room, filling out paperwork to abort this baby, and ending the struggle of being a teenage parent.

I imagined what my life would be like not only in the present but five and ten years down the road if I went through with either option. Both scenarios flowed to nowhere and nothing. I did not see a childless, successful woman working hard at a career, nor did I see a person partying and continuing the life I had been living pre-pregnancy. The imaginings would not lead to any pictures of what my life would be like. No matter how hard I focused on imagining a future without a child—through adoption or abortion—a childless future was an absolute blank.

In that moment, as I worked to get the comments from Darcie and Mom out of my mind, the little flame inside me suddenly flared as if doused with gasoline. I was going to burn so hard that the world would know. I told myself: "Teresa, you need to do this for yourself and… you MUST do this to break the cycle of dysfunction in your family."

From that moment on, I began carrying a torch. A torch that symbolized the perseverance that is related to resilience and determination.

Hyena

And on a day we meet to walk the line
And set the wall between us once again.
We keep the wall between us as we go.
To each the boulders that have fallen to each.
—Robert Frost

I didn't like it when they got her to the table. I knew they were up to something. I know they meant well. Here she was, totally excited about the future—making a future from something she really didn't foresee or choose—and there they were trying to do their best to shelter her from pain they believed would be ahead.

Yet my Teresa showed grace and courage—at sixteen. She sat and listened to them. Their suggestions did not take into consideration the bond she already had with her child.

She became more determined than ever. It would be unrealistic to think the flame didn't dim in various storms, but her resolve made it so it would never go out. She'd experienced a shitty childhood, but it would strengthen her foundation of compassion and understanding for others who had experienced difficult times. It was through the resilience and determination she showed each time she was exposed to a dysfunctional arm of her family that would allow her to become unmesswithable.

Townhouse

We settled into home. Nick attended every appointment for the baby and even took Lamaze classes with me. Nick's mom came along as well because she worked in the clinic where they were held.

Our drive and tenacity—resilience and determination—appeared to put my family at ease. I was going to do exactly what I said—break the cycle of dysfunction.

Mom and Dad saw the fire in me—a determination that they had never seen before. I likened it to the 1825 Miramichi fire that burned over three million acres of forest.

Sometimes low growing underbrush needs to be cleared, and the forest floor has to be rid of its debris so that the soil can be renewed and establish a new generation of trees.

I was going to burn dysfunction to the ground so that new relationships could grow, and communication could thrive.

I'd never been a morning person. But once I felt safe as well as determined, I'd slowly float into consciousness, safe, warm and snuggly, wrapped in my blankets, while the clomping of footsteps down the stairs became the first sounds of the day for me. This was the morning routine for Nick. Working early morning hours at the grocery store in the produce department kept him busy and productive. Through hard work, dedication, and ungodly hours, Nick had proven not only to himself but to our families, that he was the man of the house. Not a single day of work was missed, no matter how tired or how sick he was. He was a true provider, excited to be the best dad he could be.

I had a job at Subway. I didn't start until ten or after. Though it allowed me to get a few extra z's after Nick left for his shift, I never took those mornings for granted. I'd fold laundry, organize drawers, set books on the shelf, and tidy our home before I left for work. I wanted everything to be perfect for our baby. Each day I found a new task to do to make sure everything was perfect. More important than our baby having the items I'd always wanted was that I wanted our baby to feel the love, commitment, and tenderness I never received. I wanted our baby to never feel alone, always knowing that, as her parents, we would climb Mount Everest, circle all the planets, and swim across every ocean to know that they were supported through any of their wildest dreams. I wanted it to pour over our baby like an aqua waterfall that fell into a beautiful, clear pool below.

As our families saw us working our tails off to get everything lined up for the baby's arrival, they started to pitch in and help. Darcie gave us a lot of our furniture; the majority of our kitchen items came from my Tonia. Dad and I would go to rummage sales on the weekends to look for other items and clothing for the baby. Our little townhome was becoming a home, and the nursery was getting stocked from all the family members on both sides of the family.

I gave new meaning to 'hot girl summer'. Sweating profusely, gasping for air, and sporting swollen ankles described me during the summer of 1999. With a due date of August 27, 1999, my third trimester aligned with the humid hell of a Minnesota summer.

The little babe in my belly had me stretched to the max; the sandman didn't visit the baby often. Acrobatic shows to rival any in Vegas took place inside me, courtesy of an incredibly active baby.

The back pain was like none other, and my appetite was that of a wild hyena's who seized her food and then escaped back to her den to beat the heat.

Birthing Suite

There were false alarms in June and July. We neared the due date of August 27th. Every day seemed to drag on and the end never was close enough. The last week of August, the doctor said everything was looking great for the baby to arrive. August 27th came and went; our little cub continued to hibernate. Plans were made to give our baby one week longer, and then induce. There were a few contractions, but they amounted to nothing.

At the beginning of September, at our next appointment, the doctor said it was time to see some sunlight and enjoy the last part of the summer as a family. We were directed to report the next day to the maternity wing of our local hospital to be induced.

Pink socks, burp rags, diapers, wipes, fresh clothes, multiple blankets, and sleepers filled the overnight bag. I was giddiness wrapped in a ball of nerves. Nick too. We were trembling with a massive mix of emotion with every step closer to the hospital doors. While we were holding hands in the elevator to the fourth floor, I began to worry about failing our baby. For almost nine months I'd assumed I could show up and do 'it' well—do parenting. Now, I wasn't so sure.

Standing barefooted on the cold hospital floor, being prepped, gown open to back, my self couldn't believe my self was there.

Before I knew it, I was connected to monitors. I made my fears go somewhere. Shit just got real. It was happening; I was going to have a baby while I was still a baby myself. A few tears slipped down my face, but I quickly wiped them away and told myself inside my head, "Teresa, get it together. Time to man up and quit being a little bitch."

And then the fire burned brighter in me for my baby.

Sixteen and a half hours of labor later our daughter was born. September 3, 1999. She was beautiful, and a healthy seven pounds seven and a half ounces. My mom and Nick's mom were present for the entire time—Nick for most. He had to excuse himself near the end when what I would describe as the dragon was released. It was like my soul escaped my body and came back into me as a fire-breathing dragon. My best friend, Janiece waited outside in the hallway. She later told me that she heard the dragon breathe fire and at that moment had looked at Nick and said, "She's here!"

I stayed in the hospital a few days. The first two days our baby didn't have a name. We'd talked for hours throughout the pregnancy, but could never decide; during pregnancy, the thought of naming our baby before seeing her was hard for me to fathom. I thought, how am I to name a little human without seeing her personality? What if the name we chose did not fit her? The only thing I knew is that I wanted to include Tammy's middle name, 'Lynn'.

I may only have been sixteen when I became pregnant, and a month away from being seventeen when I gave birth to my baby, but I was still able to capture in my mind the process of change I'd been through and was going through.

Something happened to me during the pregnancy, when I gave birth, and after I gave birth. To me, it is the story of my transformation. It examples how we are unaware of what hangs in the balance between life and death, how incredible our journey is.

This little soul and I had connected for nine months. I'd felt her lack of rest, her constant movement, and her energy. This was her prebirth communication to me. All through my pregnancy, she was communicating with me. I just did not understand what she was trying to tell me.

Even though I had not planned the pregnancy, I knew the universe had planned it for me—I just didn't know the reason.

Once my baby was on my chest, the volume of her message was like a hurricane—one powerful enough to move the Gulf of Mexico clear onto the coast of Florida. Her 'being' and 'communication' shifted my world. I felt an overwhelming sensation as if someone was touching the deepest part of my heart, strumming the tinniest capillaries with magical powers, while softly whispering 'follow your dreams.'

I had always had dreams. They came from being alone so often while Mom was working evening shifts and Dad was sleeping for his overnights. I'd watched a lot of television that involved travel, and I marveled over the places I could go.

Detroit Lakes did not speak big city; its first language was small town, and hunters and fishers from all over America listened to it. But young people who saw themselves in sophisticated cities, and high-rises, who pictured themselves under giant, lit billboards, were deaf to Detroit Lakes' voice.

Small towns often influence its young to run away or move away. Television shows encourage big moves as well.

I'd imagined myself in a high-rise apartment overlooking the city—a city like New York. In my mind, I'd dressed up and gone out with my girlfriends a thousand times in the Big Apple. I'd walked the streets to my corporate job and stopped to get a bottle of wine on the way home; the busy life of a city girl, including the importance of having a highly sought after job and being connected to other women I could call my sisters.

Thank you, David Letterman, for the opening to your show, your guests, and bringing the big city to a small town.

From my hospital bed, my swaddled little miracle in my arms, The Letterman Show flashed across my mind, it's iconic montage of the city in its introduction. I repeated 'New York' a few times to myself. But it sounded too unusual as a name. I thought about the parts of the city and places nearby: Poughkeepsie, Ithaca, Newburgh, and Schenectady. They sounded even worse. Suddenly, bright marquees of Broadway shows appeared in my head.

"She will be called Brook Lynn," I said.

Nursery

The first few months as a mom with Brook Lynn were not the easiest. In my head, I thought we'd walk along the beach in the cool air with Brook Lynn bundled up. I pictured that we'd go to the park and be surrounded by joyful children who would offer me a vision of what the future looked like—for when I could push her on the swings. I dreamed of playing patty cake and singing 'head and shoulders, knees and toes'.

Instead, I held—because I could not put her down or she'd scream—a colicky baby almost all day and night, trying to sooth her. Diapers, spit-up, laundry, feedings made it so that I didn't even know day from night. I'd lie on the couch every moment I could, with her on my chest.

In the moments of silence, I'd think about where I needed to go in life, for me and for her, and for Nick. I was content in the space I was in but feeling the desire to be more. Nick worked at the grocery store; I took care of Brook Lynn.

The yearning for more grew; every moment of yearning was interrupted by crying and screaming. A hungry baby, needing a diaper change, would end my moments of daydreaming for more. Concerned this was going to be my reality, that I would be like this forever—in this townhouse, living paycheck to paycheck, going to rummage sales, and paying for our food with 'food stamps', threw me into a panic.

I wanted to live a life of being a mom and be able to provide my child with opportunities and, yes, 'things'. I wanted to take her on trips, and to be able to afford to put her in lessons she might want to take. I wanted to give her a life of wonder.

These thoughts and emotions popped up regularly throughout the first year of Brook Lynn's life. Not because I wasn't happy being a mom. I loved being a mom. I just wanted to be a mom and be a more financially stable parent.

Nick was happy doing what he was doing. Going to work every day, coming home to his family. I saw little desire of him wanting more. He seemed okay with mediocre.

Room for Betrayal

As I began filling out applications for jobs, and even working some, I began to feel pretty disappointed in myself, a failure in life. I didn't take into account I was only seventeen.

I told myself not finding the right employment was my fault. I was upset with myself because I'd bounced between jobs, trying to find one that would work for a mom of an infant.

I wanted to help with the bills. Nick worked early in the morning, so I looked for a part time job that I could work at when he was home. I applied at a gas station as a clerk. It was in front of Tim's house—Mom's eldest child. It was walking distance from our townhouse. When I went to speak with the manager they seemed just as enthusiastic about me working there as I was. They understood I had a newborn and seemed amiable to the shifts I'd like to fill.

When I left, the manager said they'd call me with a start date— essentially, I'd already been hired. I was excited and wanted to tell Mom and Dad. I walked into their house with a bounce in my step. "I think I got a job," I said. There was a huge smile on my face.

Mom and Dad never said the things a person who is their child or their adopted child would want to hear after they

173

received good news. There was never anything like, 'Good job' or 'That's great'.

The first thing Dad said was, "Where at?"

I told him the gas station in front of Tim's house. I explained they were nice and would work with my schedule so I could be home when I was needed to take care of Brook Lynn.

He followed that with a straight face and an 'oh'. Then he continued to watch television.

I don't recall Mom said anything at all. She may have just followed Dad's lead.

A few days passed. I decided to pick up the phone and call the gas station. I remember the conversation as if it was yesterday.

"Hi, this is Teresa. I haven't heard back from you on a start date and was wondering if you had time to get me scheduled for training?"

A moment of silence. Too long of a moment for comfort.

"I was told not to hire you. Your brother, Tim, comes in here a lot. He said you're not a good person and I'd be making a mistake hiring you." The man spoke confidently, strongly, like there was serious meaning behind the words, as if he was one step from accusing me of being a terrible person.

Tears began to run down my face. I held back the cracking in my voice and managed to say, "Okay. Thank you."

I hung up the phone and began to sob. The hurt and feeling of failure swept over my body. I felt completely let down by the people who should have been by my side; there was no interest or investment. The sheer audacity for someone to sabotage someone else trying to better themselves was devastating.

Tim's need to have this kind of power over me only solidified my views on him. I didn't know why he would do such a thing, but as I got older and was informed of many things about his life it all started to make sense.

From that point of betrayal, I avoided any interaction with Tim. If I went to Mom and Dad's place and his vehicle was there, I'd drive right by. If he ever showed up when I was at Mom and Dad's, I'd leave through one door as he'd come through the other.

Tim knew I was avoiding him. The times I could not avoid him such as holiday gatherings, he'd make sure to profess arrogantly and loudly: "You were adopted, and not even part of this family." He was an adult saying this. "If it wasn't for my parents, you would be a bigger loser." Every chance he got to tear me down with the fact I was adopted he would. I found it odd that he kept bringing up my adoption.

After Mom died with her secret, others revealed it. Tim had been adopted too. By Dad.

Again, I took the time to think about Tim's situation. Tim always knew Dad had adopted him. The rest of us 'kids' did not. He had not known his biological father. He was the biological child of Carol. Perhaps this knowledge—and the pressure of his circumstances of how he joined the family and it being kept a secret—affected him in that he had to survive a perceived abandonment of his birthfather.

I wondered if this was his ego coming into play; a form of protection that is fed and grows throughout the life of someone whose security was threatened, let alone their position as eldest child.

Yet it was dizzying for me to understand because he was and remained Dad's prized child. Their time together always appeared to be deeply cherished. Tim's admiration for Dad equalled Dad's obvious joy of having a son like Tim.

*****

On betrayal and the present;

I know forgiveness is something that is done for the peace of the person who has been hurt. I get that. And I have reached a certain peace within. Peace requires the establishment and maintenance of strong boundaries.

I don't understand why anyone would do what Tim did to me. I spent hours—probably too many—dissecting the reasons he may have done this. I've concluded that there are some things we will never know, but that we can learn from those actions taken against us by setting boundaries and choosing our own tribe, and by never lowering ourselves to that level of harming someone else—especially a kid.

Years later, I am still disturbed by what Tim did. I often wonder how he even knew I'd applied for the job. Some hurts hang around longer than others… and that's okay because it is human.

Classrooms

The start of a new century also marked an important year for me. I began taking college courses at our local technical college. Other than the benefit of further education, the upside was that there was childcare provided for their students' little ones. I was able to attend these classes and take Brook Lynn to childcare in the same building. I could stop by to check on her in between classes and on my lunch break. I was never too far away from her. I enrolled in general classes before I decided on a career path. School came easily for me; excelling in school was what I did best. I had always enjoyed learning. As a mom with new responsibilities, my passion to learn increased even more. I loved feeding my brain. Learning kept me accountable to myself, stretched my brain, and made me feel connected, needed, and wanted. I felt great about completing assignments—I did so with a dedicated excellence and received high marks. Even though I was an adult, having a teacher enthusiastic about my work was the acknowledgement I'd always wanted… always needed.

College is where I began to find my true powers. It allowed me to glimpse freedom, and it gifted me the ability to dream big.

As the year moved on, I finished general studies and moved to the Legal Secretary Program. I was still influenced by that first encounter in grade four with Officer E when he presented the DARE program; I knew I needed to do something in the legal field. Detroit Lakes, being as small as it is, only offered Legal Secretary programs.

I excelled in the program. I embraced learning about the laws, how to draft paperwork for estates, civil law, and even criminal law. Toward the end of my program, the college assisted us with finding jobs and writing resumes to obtain a job in legal offices. I was ready to graduate and begin working in a law office. This brought me excitement and a lot of daydreaming about working in a prestigious law firm in New York City one day.

Graduation from college after two years of attending every class, excelling, and getting fantastic grades was a proud moment for me. I was excited for where the degree would take me, and how much more it would provide for our family. Things were looking up. I remember going to pick up my cap and blue gown. That day I went through the doors with another young female I met in the program who became a dear friend, and later my neighbor in the same townhouses.

I was on cloud nine.

I was so proud of myself at the ceremony.

Not a single person from my family attended. Mom and Dad did not feel it necessary to watch me cross the stage, cheer my accomplishments, share their pride, witness me receive my diploma.

It was a gut punch.

I'd promised my parents early in my pregnancy that I would not do what my biological mom did to them. I'd never take off and leave my child for them to raise. I promised them I would work hard and make something of myself. I promised them I would finish school and take responsibility for myself. I had accomplished so much during the pregnancy and the two years following, and yet it didn't seem to move them, emotionally, an inch.

I remained confused as to how I might please them so that they would show their affection. When people have had a tough time as a kid, then find themselves achieving as an adult, they want to have people celebrate them when they reach worth milestones. Yes, that person can celebrate themselves—and I certainly recognized the maturity in myself and was proud of myself. But there was a frustration that came from being grateful for having been provided for, and wishing that those who had provided for me could have been at the celebration. It left me thinking that the fact they weren't there was directly linked to the difficult times I'd had as a child and teen.

The Office

Not long after graduation, Nick and I moved to Fargo, North Dakota. We moved into a small, main floor apartment of a house. Nick began working day labor in hopes to find something permanent. After many applications being filled out, resumes sent and interviews. I landed a job at a law firm in the city. I remember interviewing with the lawyer of this firm and being eager to work in his firm. During the interview he told me I would start out at the bottom and needed to work my way to the top. This is something I knew a lot about. Working hard was what I did. Proving myself was all too familiar to me. After proving myself, working hard, I would then be able to assist with the legal documents of the firm. Assisting in case briefs of depositions, contracts and testimony was what I wanted. Preparing court documents, assisting lawyers in collecting legal and factual documents, and dictation for the lawyers was where I saw myself. This lawyer told me I had promise and drive, and that in no time I would be his right-hand person.

I wanted to prepare myself for my first days of work and show up sharp. I had an image of how a professional would dress. I'd seen it when The Letterman Show filmed the streets of New York City. Although there was no money to make this happen,

I asked around and was told to try a program called 'Dress for Success'. The program included an application process which consisted of questions about a person's goals, desires, and current job situation. I was able to get through it quickly and head to the room of clothes where assistants helped with selections. Each person was allowed to choose three work outfits.

I had a completely different idea of what the room would look like. Naïve me, I expected top-notch clothing that would allow me to stand out above all others. Sadly, I was mistaken. The room was huge, dimly lit with multiple racks of clothing. The whole place smelled musty; the clothes had time traveled. The assistants behaved as if living out a scene in Pretty Woman. None of what they gave me—dresses and skirts—were my idea of how I wanted to look when I walked into my new job on day one. I settled on some dress slacks, blouses, and a pair of black shiny wedge shoes to pull the office look together.

Day one at the new job saw me filled with enthusiasm. Ready to climb the ladder. I entered through the back door and stopped at the attorney's office to find out who I would be job shadowing. He laughed ever so slightly and said, "Oh, no. You're in the basement."

Little girl me still thought I'd be in an office with someone waiting to mentor me. I was sadly mistaken.

At the bottom of the stairs was a large desk piled high with books, boxes, and paperwork. The lady at this desk wore jeans and t-shirt. This was the wife of the lawyer. Four cubicles surrounded her desk. To get to them I had to wade through lose papers and boxes overflowing with paperwork. My desk was covered in empty food containers and mouse droppings.

I asked myself: what did I get into? This is not what they show on the television!

I discovered the pristine law office was on the main floor. The basement was a side hustle for unpaid medical debts. A cross between Walter Matthau in Grumpy Old Men and Steven Tyler from Aerosmith briefly trained me.

I did not get to use my college skills, but the job paid pretty well for the area and was close to our apartment. I stuck it out for a year, never missing a day; ended up being their most successful debt collector. There was never any talk about moving up to doing the legal aspects. If I brought it up, the wife just became angry that I wanted to be upstairs. Lesson learned, always look in the basement.

Do you want fries with that?
It is not funny.
Work is work.
Some work is harder,
and made even more difficult by the
attitude of others about that work.

Nick continued to work at day labor, and I applied and was hired at the McDonalds right across the street from our apartment. The days were bleak, my fire was dimmed. I felt defeated and let down by my first employer. Plus, Nick was just going through the motions. Anyone could tell he was dissatisfied with his current working situation. Drinking overtook him and drug use, beyond marijuana, began.

We spiraled and began using cocaine regularly. Down and down the path signposted as 'Inevitable'.

Life was still about raising Brook Lynn, but the drugs and alcohol ran a close second. This went on for a few months. We partied hard, went to work, then repeated the partying. Our apartment started to become the spot for loser friends to come and do cocaine, drink, and party.

While a daughter fell asleep in her bedroom watching VHS tapes of Blues Clues, her parents abused drugs and partied. I saw our lives as a movie that is not even me but a daughter and her parents. I had to turn it around.

Then, one day I saw Shelly.

In the mirror.

After months of being tired of not being able to get our next fix, and after losing our only vehicle to repossession, I hated who I'd become.

I started seeing Shelly when I wasn't looking in the mirror.

Reset

Trouble continued in successive waves while sirens sounded in my head. I could see that, within a short time, my world would be reduced to rubble. When I closed my eyes, I saw everything I'd worked for flattened, and giant holes in the ground. Everything would be destroyed except for one treasure. There was a beacon of light that looked at me through the carnage: Brook Lynn.

I would not be Shelly.

I put a stop to it all.

I opened my eyes and chose to restart. I chose to love my daughter and to leave those who didn't share the same goals and aspirations. I chose to move forward and build a better life.

No more giving up, no more drugs, just pure motivation. I needed to find myself and follow my dreams.

The journey to those dreams would be exceedingly long and wearisome, but I had to grow up some more, and be the mother I needed to be.

I waged war on everyone around me. I was angry at the father of my child, and with Mom and Dad for not fighting for me, showing me love, supporting me through the years when I felt 'less than', unimportant, and truly unloved. I was frustrated at the father of my child for dragging me into a life of drugs and alcohol, and for being complacent. I wanted him to have the same motivations as me. In my mind, he'd allowed the both of us to be like our drug user friends—no jobs, not fighting for the both of us to be better. At the height of my blame and the lowest of my love, I even felt upset with Brook Lynn for always needing me and wanting me.

We lost the apartment. Nick went back to Detroit Lakes. I was in a sink or swim position; sinking was not an option—I have always been afraid of drowning.

The truth showed itself. The person I was most angry with was myself. I'd been a follower. I'd allowed myself to turn away from my true self. I was livid with myself for giving in and for giving up. For abandoning my dreams. For being less then the mom I wanted to be.

I would not be Shelly. I would not be anyone except me. I knew what needed to be done, and I focused on doing it through my higher self. It had to start, or re-start, with me. And it did.

I was able to build Brook Lynn's security through rebuilding my own life.

There is a fine balance to living life in a healthy way. It involves knowing what to hold on to and what to let go of, and when. One thing is for sure, if you don't leave the past behind you, you can never make room for the present or the future. I had to remind my self many times that leaving the past behind didn't mean I didn't care about someone or something anymore. I just needed to appreciate every experience for what it was teaching me, and all the gifts it brought me to learn and grow.

Building our new normal, brick by brick from the ground up, was going to be one intensive operation, and I was not a stone mason, but I knew I could make it happen.

I gave up drugs. I moved into public housing. I got a job at a local bar as a server. I was fortunate to find a wonderful daycare that would take Brook Lynn in the evenings and on into the early morning hours so I could make a living. I disliked working evenings and being away from Brook Lynn. I enjoyed our evening dinner time, cuddles and bedtime routine. The arrangement was the best thing to do; to be with her during the day and forge a path for us. We both sacrificed, Brook Lynn and me. After a few months, I was able to start saving. I could pay our bills and put some money away.

I was still fighting hard, and my airway was still above water. I knew I was swimming in the right direction. I would not drown. Even though I was likely swimming upstream, I would not drown.

Time passed, and I continued to work hard. Nick's little sister contacted me and wanted to come and stay with me. She was around twelve and wanted to stay for the summer. Her being with me allowed me to cut back on childcare costs as she would be able to watch Brook Lynn at home while I was at work in the evenings. During the day, when I was there, she'd have free time to escape whatever she was going through back in Detroit Lakes.

Brook Lynn loved having her aunt around, and so did I. She was a great help; we were able to establish a great friendship that would last a lifetime. More than a year passed; I was still working at the bar. Nick's sister came back and forth during the school year. Then one day she decided she'd stay. She'd get her GED and find work.

Meanwhile, Mom and Dad started to see how I was handling it all by myself. I'd visit them regularly and I'd talk to Dad about my wish to become a police officer. That desire had been with me since the DARE presentation in grade four—I'd been interested in legal studies and entered the legal administration program because of that.

While lawyer crossed my mind a few times, the logistics seemed too demanding to handle for a single mom raising her child.

Hyena

"In three words I can sum up everything
I've learned about life:
it goes on."
—Robert Frost

It did go on. It will always go on.

We plant a seed, and we know we have to wait while nature is working away at changing that seed into a flower or a vegetable. We get that we will need to wait. It comes naturally to us to wait for what we planted to grow. There is a process to the garden growing. We don't see all the inside work, but we trust it is happening.

I could see the garden of Teresa. I was gardening in that garden, planting seeds by envisioning outcomes, and trusting in the knowing I was part of an energy system that was mostly unknown by humans… I could hardly understand it myself as a novice guide, and in the form of a hyena at that.

I had knowledge that I'd been a hyena on the earth, and that I knew everything hyena, and that I had evolved and been sent to Minnesota. This was nothing more than an invisible boundary created by humans who had marked out a geographical area and might well at some point in the future mark it out again and call it something else.

Time was such a solid concept in Teresa's world. Not so much in mine. But seeds were everywhere in the form of energy, waiting to grow new ideas and new people.

In Teresa's world, seeds were planted in the way of obtaining an education and making plans that would involve investment of labor; there would be waiting, and weeding, and then there would be results.

Teresa had the mindset of a gardener, a hard working one. The plot she had to work on was filled with rocks and the soil was not the best for growing things. She had to clear her land and add to her soil. Every time she did something to grow a beautiful thing, some big-booted brute would come and crush the seedlings.

When her brother talked to the gas station guy who had promised Teresa a job, I must have been looking the other way because I cannot imagine myself, despite my peacefulness, letting him get away with that. It's still a tough one to deal with. And I want to be as compassionate with Tim as I am with Shelly, but it was such a betrayal.

Still, even with that duplicity from her uncle who she had always called a brother, Teresa moved on. And she went to school, and she served at the law firm in that shitty basement for a long time. She worked hard and was not going to let that work be for nothing.

Teresa persevered and learned to curate all the parts of her life as if it were a gallery; each phase was an amazing exhibition. I loved and love her for that.

I'm over-metaphorizing here, but think of the backtracking in life, the hiccups, the bad seasons in the garden like this:

Stopping at a traffic light may inconvenience you or slow your journey. But if you didn't, then there'd be no order or even traffic pattern and you would crash. Plus, you'd miss thinking about your route. It's the same with stopping to consider events and future actions in life. Stopping is not a weakness. It is a necessary part of success. Sometimes stopping, and even taking a few steps back, serves to remind us of what is truly important. Regression can help us remember what it is we DON'T want. Teresa and Nick were young and had been defeated by a system that isn't completely supportive of young parents—it is almost a punitive system that makes life more difficult than it needs to be. Teresa's difficulties and temporary step back into destructive behaviors allowed her to see what she didn't want and then to regroup. It served as fuel.

Even as a guide, I had to stop and evaluate what was happening, go over my role, 'our' route, appreciate how far we'd come, and anticipate detours.

Renovation

Let me catch you up: I'd moved away from the lifestyle I'd fallen back into. I was working, I was good mother providing for Brook Lynn... my parents were impressed with how I was handling it. I just knew I needed a career instead of a job.

I spent a few months looking into the logistics of attending school to become a police officer. The school in Alexandria was a two-hour drive from where I lived and, of course, two hours back. Four hours of commuting on top of an eight-hour day of classes. I knew I couldn't give up my apartment on account of it being public housing—I might never get it back. If I did give it up, the apartments in Alexandria came at a premium in price, and daycares were full. I was stuck. Again.

I kept working and dreaming. Mom and Dad knew what I had discovered about the housing and daycare situation. I'd updated them so they knew I was still working on making a difference in my life. And that of Brook Lynn.

I was determined not to be Shelly.

One weekend I drove to Mom and Dad's in my rust bucket of a car. The two of them were sitting in the living room, smoking cigarettes, watching television. Nothing new except I was aware that Mom had started to show signs of decline in her health. She was retired but was not that active and hardly went out.

We watched television together—not a lot of words exchanged, as usual, until it was time for Brook Lynn and me to leave. As I left through the back door, Mom and Dad followed me around the side of the house and out to the driveway.

I was kind of watching over my shoulder, knowing they were following me. It was odd.

Then Dad's voice broke the silence. "Teresa, CATCH!"

I turned around and set of car keys hit me square in the chest. "What's this?" I asked.

"This is for you and Brook Lynn," said Dad. The two had retreated to the back porch. Both were smiling.

Dad had waited to throw the keys until I was standing next to Mom's 1997 Mercury Tracer. I had always loved this sea-green vehicle. It was comfortable and attractive. I had been driving a 1985 Plymouth Reliant that was rusted out, had torn seats, and lacked any kind of power. The Mercury Tracer was a luxury vehicle to me.

I couldn't believe it was happening. Were they giving it to me?

"What will Mom drive?" I asked. "Why are you doing this for me? What did I do to deserve this?" I also wondered how I would afford it because I wasn't sure it was a full give.

They explained that with Mom no longer working they didn't need two cars. They wanted me to have a reliable car for Brook Lynn and for me—a safe car that could help me follow my dreams of becoming a police officer.

"We want to take some of the burden off you," said Dad. "All we ask is that you pay us $107.00 a month until the balance of the car is paid."

Why they decided that amount is unknown to me; there was about seven-thousand outstanding on their loan. Perhaps they wanted me to take on some responsibility but not take on the whole monthly loan amount.

I began emptying my rust-bucket and transferring items to the sea-green dream. As I did that, a friend of Dad's pulled up and handed Dad five hundred dollars. Dad looked at me. "Thanks for the downpayment," he said. Then he laughed and kept giggling. "I sold your car, for the down payment. My friend is buying it for his son."

My debt was reduced to sixty-five hundred on the spot. I was filled with happiness for so many reasons. I finished putting Brook Lynn's car seat in the 'new to me' car, then I gave Mom and Dad each a hug and thanked them.

Both my parents grew ten feet in my eyes that day.

With this support and encouragement, I felt like a whole new person—more motivated than I had ever been.

The Alexandria Technical College offered two programs for police officers. One was a two-year program for people out of high school or adults with no degree. The other option was police academy only for those who already had a two-year degree. What would be required is for me to attend three full-time semesters to obtain my law enforcement diploma. The fall and spring academy was on offer—if I did not make the decision to apply in the next two months, I'd have to wait an entire year to apply again.

I have always been a person who jumps on things when they are in front of me. I also knew that a lot could distract me in the next year and stop me from going altogether.

The next week I applied at the Police Academy in Alexandria, Minnesota. I opted for this route as I already had an AAS degree. I submitted my application and fee then I waited impatiently. A couple weeks went by, and I heard nothing. This is when I began calling and calling because I needed to know if I was accepted so I could arrange childcare, housing, and funding to make it happen. The other reason was because I was excited to know if I was finally going to be able to start bettering Brook Lynn's and my life. I was told that the committee was meeting this week to go through all the applications. Documents would be sent out the following week. I couldn't fathom waiting another week to get the news, but this was another situation I could not control, so continued to wait impatiently.

The following week I checked the mail ten times a day. Monday came and went, Tuesday crawled by, still no letter; nothing but bills and junk mail. Wednesday came in like a sloth—no letter. When Thursday arrived, I decided if the letter didn't arrive, I'd burst. I was on the verge of tears because I'd built up so many negative thoughts—each day I'd told myself they don't want me; I have nothing to offer. I am not good enough to be a police officer. Maybe its not meant for me. I am not strong enough. I am not intelligent enough.

Picture a sad puppy with drooping ears at a window, watching all the cars go by, watching dogs with their owners on the way to the park. This was a clear picture of how I looked on that Thursday.

When the postal worker came into view, I jumped up, ran up the stairs, and zoomed out the door. I flung open the door and barreled down the sidewalk like a wild stallion. The mailman didn't know what had hit him, that's how much enthusiasm I had. I snatched the mail he was going to hand to me nicely.

Pages from a K-Mart flyer alerted me to a Sega Genesis for $189.00—with two bonus games. It dropped to the ground with a Columbia House—Eight CDs for a penny. I tossed the rest of the mail until I had the golden envelope—though it wasn't gold, it was to me; the return address of Alexandria Technical College holding my attention. I wanted to open the envelope right there in front of the confused mailman. The reason I didn't was because, if the contents were bad news, I knew I'd break down in front of him and the other neighbors whose attention I'd attracted.

I left the flyers on the sidewalk, ran into the front entryway of the public townhome, and shut the door to the world around me.

"If I don't get accepted it will be okay." I prepared myself for the worst. "Do I really want to go through all this trouble to go to school? Do I really think I am worth it? I won't make a good police officer anyway. I couldn't go, I must take care of Brook Lynn." I told myself all these things so that I could manage the 'we regret to inform you' that I believed was highly probable.

I stood in the entryway, frozen with self-doubt. Then I slid my finger between the top edges of the envelope until I was able to pull out the letter.

The first thing I noticed when I unfolded the first third of the trifolded page was the school logo and address embossed across the top. An official letterhead. I unfolded it one more time and I saw the opening 'Dear Teresa'. One more unfolding.

Congratulations you have been selected as a candidate for the Transitional Program for Police Officers at Alexandria Technical College.

I began to scream aloud. "I freaking did it. I freaking did it" A rush of adrenaline took over. I began shaking. And that's when the crying began. This was new for me. I rarely cried. Crying was for wimps and only reserved for the spankings I received as a child. Even then, I would often hold back tears. Tears were a sign of weakness. Not today though.

All through my life, all I'd ever done was look for acceptance. That day was a day of acceptance.

When reality kicked in, I continued to read the letter. To be accepted did not guarantee a spot at school. Acceptance meant that I met the criteria they were looking for and now I could move on for the physical from a doctor, pass a physical fitness test, and then face an interview panel to be evaluated as to whether I was a right fit.

Interview Room

The hard work began immediately.

Some applicants worry about their fitness level, others about their academic capabilities. Each of these kinds of people can train to get fitter, or study and upgrade their skills.

I'd had a short but colorfully chaotic life. I was immediately concerned about how my past would influence an organization's decision-making. I couldn't 'train' or 'study' my past experiences away.

The physical exam cleared me for the physical agility test which comprised push-ups, sit-ups, suicide runs, jumping, and a mile run. I had been an athlete—a runner—through middle school and a little bit of high school. The fitness test was child's play for me.

The part that sent me to hell and back a thousand times in my mind was the fifty-plus page document of questions that had to be answered. Those answers would affect my evaluation.

The questions covered topics I did not want to touch: family dynamics, childhood upbringing, drug use, criminal activity, mental health status. These questions would be asked in a face-to-face interview.

When I reviewed them in the privacy of my own home, I

could see they started with easy ones.

What is it that drew you to pursue a career in Law Enforcement?

Officer E made a good impression on me in grade four. He continued to be involved in my school and community. I was inspired by the community policing and his investment. Watching him gave me hope for my own future.

How well do you deal with stressful situations?

It was difficult to share that the proof of my being able to deal with stressful situations was also a source of shame.

I answered: I handle situations of stress extremely well. I had a child at sixteen. I have been on my own since then and have supported myself and completed two years of college.

How would you describe yourself?

Driven, outgoing, strong, intelligent. Also fearful, not worthy, unloved, mostly empty.

Have you committed Arson?

No.

Have you ever been paid for sexual activity?

No

Have you ever been involved in or distributed child pornography?

No.

After the initial questions, I was on a roll, for a little bit. I remember asking myself, is this all they've got? If that's the case, I thought, I'll ace this interview. So, I turned the page and kept going... as if I'd ever committed arson.

Then it got a little more personal.

Have you ever had any contact with a police officer?

I skipped over it, giving myself time to think of an answer that would not disqualify me. I mean, everyone's had contact with a police officer, haven't they? And Officer E was present at school, and active in community policing.

Have you ever been detained by a police officer?

This one took me down memory lane. Did the time I ran into a river and then lay wet and freezing between a downed tree and garage count? Or how about being placed into a squad car, handcuffed, while a friend escaped from the front—still handcuffed. Then there was that Greyhound bus trip across country when I was thirteen, and those Montana Troopers.

Have you ever been charged with a crime, arrested, or convicted of a crime?

Charged, no. Convicted, no.

Then I began to think about what constituted an arrest. I'd had to go to court as a minor with a citation. Did that count as an arrest? How naïve was I?

Have you ever been questioned as a suspect in a crime?

My mind went off on me again. "Does getting plummeted, tossed to the ground, handcuffed and shoved into a squad car when you are sixteen and didn't know what sex was until your friend told you but that was already after you'd had it and so you were trying to tell the guy you slept with that you are now pregnant happened at the exact same time as a police raid count?"

How would you describe your family dynamic?

Another door opened to my past as I thought about how to answer it. A part of me instantly defaulted to: pretty fucked up. But another part of me balanced it all with the progress I'd made: my childhood wasn't horrific. I'd had a roof over my head. My parents, who were really my grandparents, but I didn't know it, did the best they could with what they had.

Have you used any illegal drugs or drugs not prescribed to you?

My God. There it was. How would I answer that I had made so many mistakes in my young life. I wanted them to see the clean me, filled with determination and resilience, who had gone to college and held down jobs, and worked hard to raise my child. Could I just say: I am not Shelly? Would they understand that? Did they really want me to talk about how many times I smoked marijuana and snorted lines of cocaine? Did they want to judge me for being a terrible mother and partying while my baby girl was watching Blues Clues in her room until she fell asleep?

Reading these questions was nerve-wracking for me. I had never—not in my whole life—talked about feelings. My family of origin never talked about life, how they felt, what they were going through. What would it be like when the police interviewers asked me these questions face-to-face?

*****

For the first time in my life, I was unable to sweep things under the rug the way I'd been taught over my twenty-years. I put down the booklet of questions. There'd be no carpet or broom in the interview room. I thought back to grade four and the beginning of my relationship with the police. How positive that had been. And how, over the years, despite my teenage rebellion, I'd not lost that inner inspiration or let go of my need to serve others.

In my sadness of believing that I'd reached the wall and that the interview would be a door closed to a dream, I failed to see how my experience would help me identify with youth, to recognize that there would be pressures and strains on kids who broke the law—I didn't see what I'd been through would allow for a compassionate officer in the community. I also didn't see how the resilience and dedication that had gotten me through all the dysfunction demonstrated great strength that would be needed in policing.

Despite my outwardly knowing the interview would determine my future and crush my dream, my inner self still pushed on. Resilience held one of my hands and Determination held the other as I dragged my story into the interview.

The interview was about two hours—an interrogation. It was as if I was in a court of law with my entire past brought up and used against me. In effect, it was.

I provided minimal information out of pure shame—I didn't want to talk about my failures in detail.

When I left the interview board, I was defeated. What other options did I have? What could I go to school for now? What could I do in the meantime to pay the bills? Was I going to be a piece of shit my entire life?

Winston Churchill said, "If you are going through hell, keep going."

I said, "I will not be Shelly. I am not Shelly."

Moving Van

It was a brisk fall morning. Brook Lynn and I were sitting on the sofa with the coffee table in front where Brook Lynn was having her breakfast when a knock-knock-knock on the door stopped us.

I opened the door to Dad. Behind him was my 'brother', Jay. Behind them were a couple of pickups with trailers attached.

"What are you doing here?" I asked them.

My brother chuckled and Dad smiled wide. "It's moving day," said Dad.

Confused, I invited them in as Brook Lynn finished up her breakfast.

Dad handed me a white envelope which had been opened. The return address was Alexandria technical College. I withdrew the letter, which was addressed to me.

The first line read: "Congratulations, you have been accepted into the Spring semester law-enforcement transitional program." Attached to the letter was a page of directions for financial aid.

For some reason, the acceptance letter had gone to Mom and Dad's address. They'd opened it. I forgave them for opening the letter because it had caused Dad's unusual joy. It became the catalyst for his planning my future.

"We got this today," he said. "Mom and I decided it is time for you to move home. We've got some trucks and trailers with us. You can start packing, start moving today."

I stood in the living room listening to him. My head was spinning. I was an independent woman with a child in my own place. What would this mean? What was about to happen? I needed to hear details of their expectations. But I never asked him. I just let the thoughts and questions cycle inside me. In that moment, inside my head, it was like a tornado was tearing through a town.

I began packing up the little things around my townhouse as my dad and brother dismantled furniture and beds and began hauling all of it out to the trailers and trucks. Within the week, I was fully moved into the basement of Mom and Dad's house in Detroit Lakes. Everything except our clothing and personal items went to storage. As I moved in, I still had no idea of their plan. Or how it would work out. Mom and Dad never discussed their plan for me or for Brook Lynn.

Finally, one morning, over coffee at the kitchen table, I asked them both, "What are we doing here, and how is it all going to work out?"

Calmly, and with conviction, Mom and Dad laid out their plans for me. I would attend school Monday through Friday at Alexandria Technical College. I would have to leave the house at five-thirty in the morning and drive the two hours to the college. Mom and Dad would get Brook Lynn up later, then feed her and get her onto the school bus. After school, they'd meet her at the bus and work on her homework and feed her supper. At that time, I'd be driving the two hours home.

Once Brook Lynn went to bed, I could work on my homework. On the weekend, I could work part time somewhere.

Yes, it would be hard. But it was three full semesters. It wasn't forever.

And, just like that, Mom and Dad became the lantern to guide me. It had only taken twenty years. I wondered, why now? I could see and feel their enthusiasm. They were enthralled with the idea of my becoming a police officer. I wondered if I was their new 'Tim'. Here they were, willing to bend over backwards: put us up in the basement and provide childcare—they'd never even offered to babysit in the past. I recall asking a couple of times for an hour or two break and they'd said that I should ask my sisters.

It was strange to suddenly feel supported. Fearful as I was, I wasn't going to say 'no'. I needed every ounce of help for this massive undertaking. Brook Lynn was my priority, and Mom and Dad had changed somewhat since my upbringing, With Mom home fulltime, and Brook Lynn going to school, and me with her as often as I could be, I knew she'd be safe.

I remain eternally grateful for what Mom and Dad did.

Pride

I was a single parent hell bent on making my dreams come true.

Financial aid was approved. I made the two-hour drive and walked into school on the first day with so much pride. I had my new backpack, notebooks, and pencils. Not to mention I was donning my new, brown polyester, school-issued police attire with a brass nametag that said 'Teresa'. I wore a black leather duty belt with handcuffs, mace, baton, and an empty gun holster around my hips. All law enforcement students had to wear this uniform to school. Everyone was expected to arrive clean, hair pulled back (for women), clean shaven (for men), and boots shined and free of blemishes. The brown polyester uniform was expected to be neatly pressed.

The thought process behind this was to take pride in how you looked. Later in my career, I learned why taking pride in how you looked plays an important role in staying alive when in situations that included arrests or questioning suspects.

I was proud. Proud of myself. I was moving ahead, creating the life I wanted for Brook Lynn and myself.

I needed to make it through three semesters. If I could survive and find a way to get through it with a sense of 'thriving for the future', then this time next year that 'hard work' would be over.

Yes, I'd be onto more hard work, but the school stage would be over. I reminded myself I'd attended and completed school when I'd been pregnant and sixteen. I knew, no matter the long drive, I could do this.

I attended college five days a week—forty hours of classroom time; windshield time was twenty hours in five days. Every ounce of free time was for homework. Lunchbreaks were never about hanging out; they were study and assignment time.

The first semester opened my eyes. My Introduction to Criminal Justice class gave me an overview of the American criminal justice system with specific roles and responsibilities of the police, courts, correction institutions, and the democratic foundations on which the systems are based. Semester one included an introduction to the criminal justice system, juvenile justice, emergency medical responder, and criminal investigations.

The schoolwork was challenging because of my schedule, but the experience of being a student of law enforcement was fascinating. I enjoyed it because I was compelled to learn about those topics. I had always loved learning. When you're passionate about something, the learning about it is easier.

On top of this, all through the first semester I learned about myself. I learned who I was. It became clear to me the kind of mother, person, community member, and officer I wanted to be. I thrived in this environment and soaked everything up like a sponge. My hard work paid off; I made the Dean's List my first semester.

Schedule

Semester two covered Minnesota statutes, and law enforcement and how it affected human behavior and community.

I am a black and white person—no grays in my area of thinking. This class allowed me to indulge in the exact laws of the state.

What I discovered, later, was that a lot of pressure is put on police officers—they are often expected to predict the future and have Xray vision to see concealed weapons. One thing that can help officers, is studying human behavior—it helps members hone the predictive part of their role. Since my early days as an officer, I've believed that police officers benefit from regular training and upgrading on the ever-evolving topic of human behavior.

The criminal procedure course blew my mind. It was one of the most difficult classes I have ever been a part of. This class examined the history of the United States Constitution and the role it played in our democracy, and the role it continues to play.

Learning about constitutional limitations over private citizens and police procedural handling of criminal cases was complex and introduced how technology has influenced public perception and information flow regarding police interaction in the community.

Every day was filled with subjects that were learnable on paper and multi-tentacled when off the page. Policing involves so much more than most realize. I wasn't even on the street yet, and I could see how communication and positive social interaction was necessary for prevention of crime and the prevention of escalation of violence.

Eventually, I found myself standing on a gun range, with duty holster wrapped around my hips, with all the same tools as before but this time the gun holster was not empty. The holster held a 9mm Glock handgun used for training purposes. At the beginning of the 8 weeks the firearm was not loaded, and we were just instructed to pull it out and put the sights on the target. We were also given instruction to "dry fire" our weapons at home.

Watching TV in my parents' basement in the evenings, Brook Lynn was in bed. I had my duty belt strapped around my hips, and empty Glock 9mm in my holster. I would pull it out and put it on target (the TV) hundreds and hundreds of times a night, to get my muscle memory built up.

Every morning we reported for physical fitness training at the butt crack of dawn—of course, I'd been up way before that for the two-hour drive. Although hard at first, I began to really enjoy our physical training and even got into the best shape I had ever been in. The love I once had for running was no longer there on the three-mile runs we did every single day. I despised running. I would rather be doing obstacle courses, dragging bodies, sit-ups, and push-ups. The reason for the runs was to build up our endurance, something I realized was necessary when I was in my law enforcement career. Endurance links to the question I have been asked the most about my training and police career:

Are police officers/potential police officers really, tased, maced, attacked by dogs, and gassed?

Yes. To all of the above. Each student eventually engaged their strength through serious testing that included being maced in the face, then having to fight off an attacker. Tasing was also a part of the training—and a reason to thank the endurance building. Another test was to sit in a small room with a handful of other students, everyone wearing a gas mask while gas was pumped into the room. Once it was, each student had to remove their mask, state their name and date of birth, without fighting for breath or vomiting.

Endurance is underrated. Along with resilience and patience, it is essential for a successful resume, and for being unmesswithable.

Hyena

"I am not a teacher, but an awakener."
—Robert Frost

She did it! My Teresa. I just wanted her to hear me cheer. Long gone were the days I would wait outside the house and watch her through a window. I was going everywhere with her, beside her. I'd sat and watched TV with Brook Lynn and Carol and Gary at their house. I'd been right at her heels when she'd left. I knew they were following her around to the driveway, but I didn't know why; I was already getting in the old rust-bucket when the keys came flying through the air and hit her square in the chest. Change of plans, I thought. I couldn't unhook Brook Lynn's car seat fast enough—I mean help Teresa change it to Carol's car.

I wished she could hear me. I knew it was huge that I could be near her. And she still brushed her legs when I was right there, as if she could feel me. And at night when she was sleeping, she'd rest her hand on me, then breathe a little easier. I figured she must know there was a presence near her; something resonating inside that was helping drive her. But no matter how much I sang with her in the car on the commute to and from school, she did not hear me.

And then in class every day—we learned so much. What a lot of rules a community of humans lives under. Mind blowing. She

210

always had her head in the assignments she'd done the night before, and part of her mind in what was coming up. Between places, I just wanted to carry her books.

At lunchtimes she worked on her homework too. She was a finely oiled machine that rarely had downtime—I did worry she wasn't getting enough sleep. I hope the lullabies helped.

First Job

It was official. I had a career ahead of me, now I just needed a job. When I graduated in the spring of 2006, I began applying to various police departments. I applied, and applied, and applied. Brook Lynn would be seven in a few months; I wanted a future for her and for me where we were established. I continued to live with Mom and Dad. While I applied, then moved to a two-bedroom place not far from them, I worked in security at a department store where I was in loss prevention. I kept applying and became a squeaky wheel—persistent in following up with the local law enforcement office.

Here's what a squeaky wheel looks like:

Even though I was a freshly graduated police academy student with, at the time, a two-year degree, and a lot of life experience, I was passed over by 20-30 police departments. At that time there was no more than two positions for every 400 applicants. I sent an application with a professionally prepared resume to the sheriff's office in my hometown. For weeks I never heard a thing, but the position of deputy sheriff remained on their website. I finally decided to call the sheriff's office and speak to someone about my resume. A male answered the phone and, as a result of our conversation, he told me he'd get my information to the sheriff, which he did. The sheriff said they were conducting interviews that week and I hadn't been selected.

A month went by; the department still had the position on their website, so I called and the same guy answered the phone. "No," he said. "We've not filled it. There haven't been any qualified applicants." I requested to be considered for the next interview boards and he said someone would get back to me. This went on for two months, with me calling every two weeks. Every time except once I spoke to the same male.

What became my final call to them went down with the same male saying, "The squeaky wheel gets the grease." I had been selected to be interviewed. When it was time, I wore a black suit, dress shoes, and I pulled my hair back into a bun. I was confident in how I looked and felt and was pleased with how my interview went with the sheriff, two other deputies, and the person I'd had all those follow-up calls with.

Ultimately, I was hired, but not in the position of deputy sheriff that had been advertised.

Here's the kicker—years later, I was given my background investigation file which had been prepared when I'd applied. Inside that file were my scores from the interview board. Everyone on the board ranked me high with no bad remarks except for the male I'd been speaking to all those times I'd called (all those times except one call). That male scored me considerably lower than everyone else. At the bottom of the page he'd written: "Don't like the way she looks. Do not hire." He ranked my appearance as a 3. Yes, there was a category for appearance.

Though I am not a person who wishes people bad things, I will say that, years later, this male faced his own challenges and karma did visit him.

The thing is, this is the "men"tality that needs to change. We need to empower men to support women. We must raise our children to understand the significance of gender respect.

As the squeaky wheel, despite that man's 'do not hire', I was hired in the summer of 2007. I was told I'd be deployed as a School Resource Officer. Although I wanted to be a road cop, I took the position and hoped that I could work my way into the male-dominated department of police officers. For the first month, I was paired with another officer—I basically sat in the passenger seat of a cruiser. When school started in September, Brook Lynn turned eight and went back to school at the private Catholic school she had been attending; I started work in the K-12 public school in town—a building which I lived a stone's throw from.

In the winter of 2007, I moved to a farmhouse in Mahnomen county, and continued working as a resource officer at the school. When the school year was over, I moved back into town, and secured a position as a deputy in the summer of 2008. I'd worked days as the resource officer, now I'd work a seven at night to seven in the morning shift and patrol the county and area as a road cop.

Looking back, it is kind of wild because I'd been inspired by Officer E when I was in grade four, and I began my career in the same way.

While I worked at the school, I built a lot of meaningful relationships with students and their parents in the community. One such friendship was with a wonderful girl, Randi, whose mom was the county social worker. We became friends and I watched her mature into a responsible adolescent.

When the school year was over and my duties changed to be a road cop on a night shift, Randi agreed to be my night nanny.

It was a positive time of life. Brook Lynn was thriving, my parents were proud of me, and I'd made many positive connections with the community through my work as a resource officer at the school. I even bought a house. Hell, I was proud of me.

Real Life

I'd learned so much through being a school support officer—the dynamics in families, the affects of peer relationships, the power of mentors and important role of teachers. I learned about myself and established a deeper sense of trust in myself. So mature was the relationship I had with myself that there were times when I could feel the presence of what some might call 'the higher self'. I'd always had intuition and 'that little voice', but it developed (almost without me knowing) while I was at the school. I could recognize those who struggled and those who thrived. I could apply that to my parenting Brook Lynn, and I could see so much—as if looking in a rearview mirror—of my own youth and childhood. It was as if a highly-productive conversation existed inside my heart and my head. One was me and one was a cheerleader-guide of sorts. The style was similar to mine, and involved four letter words and quirkiness, yet the cheerleader-guide side was motivating and analytical. More and more, I'd lean on it for decision making, and to review my conduct for the purpose of growth and future.

Yes, I'd wanted to go out on the road immediately and, yes, it was totally sexist and unfair that there was a male influence that put me in that school position, but hindsight allows for a person to see and evaluate the value of life circumstances.

Not only was I able to help others in positions I'd once been in as a young child and teenager, I was able to develop myself and become more informed and well-rounded. I was also able to meet Randi and her mother—Randi became a key part of Brook Lynn's and my life, would be part of my extended family, and be the consistency Brook Lynn and I needed for me to develop as an officer and for Brook Lynn to thrive in school.

From the end of school in 2008, until the late summer of 2012, I served as a police officer on the night shift and attended, in person, hundreds of crises calls, and dealt with resolving many more people-problems on the phone.

This brought out the absolute best in me and paved the way for my future training as a detective. It also took me to dark places every officer has been. Places where they must face and deal with the fear of being killed on the job.

My first months were busy with road accidents, driving offenses, alcohol and drug related calls, domestic abuse situations—everything a rural community deals with in the course of people experiencing trauma from bad luck or bad decisions. I filed away every call, learning about communication from each, and developing a balance that included compassion and upholding the law to keep everyone in the community safe.

The Shooting

On the morning of February 18, 2009, I woke to a ringing phone. It was still Minnesota-winter dark, and I knew it was probably around minus thirty outside.

"Teresa," said a senior officer who was an investigator. "There's a shooting happening, right by your house."

"Right by my house?"

"Get there. Every available officer needs to get there."

I wasn't even dressed yet.

"Teresa," the investigator said.

"I'm getting ready as fast as I can," I said into the phone.

"Teresa, Chris Dewey has been shot."

Time stood still. Chris was the closest thing I had to a partner. My heart broke. Then time sped up. I grabbed a pair of socks. The wrong ones. The kind you wear with dress pants. Thin. Not socks you'd wear to spend time outdoors.

I put on those thin socks. I raced to finish getting dressed.

A standoff with the gunman or gunmen was occurring steps from where I was—within two blocks. Moments before, I'd been warm and comfortable in my bed. Brook Lynn was down the hall, warm and comfy in hers.

One of my most vivid memories from the event that followed was how cold it was and, specifically, how cold my feet were. As I gathered my clothes, I made a phone call to a trusted caregiver. I woke Brook Lynn and assured her that someone was minutes away. The schools would be shut down if there was an active shooter in the community.

The cold air froze me as soon as I stepped outside. My cruiser coughed to a start, and I swallowed hard because Brook Lynn would be alone for a short time because I'd been called out, and the bigger fear that she could be alone a lot longer because I might not come home. Serve the people or serve your daughter. This is the issue of every single parent who works the front lines in the shoes of a first responder. Minutes later I was at the scene, and it was still active. At least the gunmen were holed up in a house, so they weren't heading to my house.

Someone I trusted would be over in a matter of minutes to be with Brook Lynn.

I focused on the task at hand, to be part of the team which had to make sure no one else was hurt.

When I arrived, Chris' body was on the pavement. I had no idea if he was dead or alive. I was briefed that there were two men, armed with weapons, in the house across the street from the house where Chris' body lay.

An ambulance pulled in at the end of the street, but the scene was not secure enough for them to proceed. However, one of the members of the medical emergency team got out of the ambulance, drove a pickup truck down the street, and loaded Chris into the back and transported him to the waiting ambulance.

Minutes later, I heard the chopper blades of a life flight helicopter and assumed that Chris would be flown from the local hospital to the major center in Fargo. This meant he was still breathing.

During all of this, law enforcement officers from my own community were in place, focused on the house in which two men had barricaded themselves. From time to time, the men opened the front door and shot at us.

Eventually, we were joined by various teams, including the bomb squad and a negotiator.

It was a scene not unlike one from a war film.

Despite the focus on the situation, every other thought was how cold I was and why hadn't I put on my thicker socks. Creativity was necessary to keep from freezing. With the opened car door as my shield, I adjusted my position, and that of the heating vents to defrost one area of my body at a time.

I had to push away the mounting sadness of Chris fighting for his life. I had to shove the potential of any of my colleagues or fellow officers on site being injured or killed during this standoff. I could not entertain that it might be me next. It just couldn't be. I was a mom. I had responsibilities.

I had sworn an oath to protect the public, and to uphold the law. This is where I belonged in this moment, and every moment after, for as many hours as it would take. Surgeons do brain surgery and do not walk out in the middle; they've taken an oath to protect life. Sometimes those surgeries are many hours long. Thank Jesus for the heaters, though they did little. They probably saved a lot of us from frostbite.

Chris had been shot once in the head and twice in the belly. And why? He'd been investigating a report of drunk driving. He'd been doing his job to keep the public safe.

The clock ticked. The standoff continued.

A person can fly from Los Angeles to New York City, take a cab and check into a hotel, in six and a half hours.

A person can go to work in the morning, take a ten o'clock coffee break, work to lunch, go out for lunch, return, and still finish a project in the afternoon and six and a half hours will have gone by.

I stood, stooped, crouched, focused, stretched, froze parts of my body and kept a vigil with my firearm pointed toward a house for six and a half hours. During that time, I was—and my colleagues—under threat of fire and fired at.

I was not alone in praying negotiators would make a breakthrough and resolve the situation—two men had basically lost it over an officer wanting to keep the street safe by stopping them from driving under the influence. The men had even attempted to steal Chris' cruiser. They'd made their way to a woman's house—the woman on whose driveway Chris was shot—and she had called 9-1-1. Then the men had gone across the street to the house that was presumed their home.

During all of this, over a basic traffic stop, an officer was now in critical condition.

Six and a half hours is time to wonder, many times, what your child is thinking. The mind goes to, is my mom coming home? It's time enough for family and friends to wonder if this is their daughter's, sister's, aunt's, uncle's, brother's, bestie's day to die.

Six and a half hours in the freezing cold, holding a rifle, and not knowing if you'll be shot at any moment, is time to question your allegiance to your job, your decision-making process, and what your future will look like if you step away. It is even enough time for your mind to be sarcastic and decide that, if you're not shot, you'll freeze to death.

One thing we didn't have time for in that six and a half hours was to get hungry, thirsty, or answer any of those critical questions. We remained engaged.

After Chris Dewey was shot, it still took six and a half hours for the negotiated surrender of the two individuals irresponsibly and horribly responsible.

When it was over, it was not over. I recall shivering in front of the heater. Calling home. Hearing Brook Lynn's voice. There were mountains of reports and paperwork related to charges and procedures. Numerous felony charges were filed as a result, including attempted murder of Chris Dewey.

Chris clung to life for several months, while his wife struggled to deal with the entire trauma of the event. In August, Chris passed away as a result of the shooting. There was so much more to this story—tragic consequences for years for Chris' high school sweetheart wife.

The charges involved included murder in the first-degree, first-degree assault, second-degree assault, and failure to render aid, Those charges were in relation to the police officers from Mahnomen County and Tribal police from the White Earth first nations.

I was one of those officers.

Yes, more than one person attempted to murder me.

I went home that day and held my child, and laughed at my socks, and tried to figure out how I would navigate my future.

That day, policework shifted for me. I loved it still, and wanted to serve, but I had more fear in me than before. I dealt with it stoically. I did not allow it to get in the way of my service. I was, however, keenly aware that my passing would affect my daughter—and I was diligent about maintaining a healthy body and mind so that I was sharp and attentive on the job.

I continued to work as a road cop, attending grisly accidents, knocking on the doors of homes in which couples fought with each other. I worked hard and I made a difference, and I raised my child, and Randi continued to stay over at night as my night nanny. I forged relationships in my personal life, even found some time to date, and I looked for opportunities where I could grow as an officer, increase my skills, and be promoted to higher ranks.

In 2012 I gave my notice to my superiors in Mahnomen County. I'd found a position in a place I could never have predicted I would work, and as far away from Minnesota as I could ever imagine.

Review of Resilience

Resilience is often confused with resistance. Resistance is for jackets and hiking boots, and tents that are in a constant state of 'trying' to keep out the harsh elements. For example: rain resistant fabric.

Resistance in life infers that we are fighting everything that is thrown at us. No one wants to do that. It is better to learn our way through life and, in those tough times (when stuff is thrown at us), draw on our resilience—our inner strengths—we developed in the past when we 'learned' from previous situations.

Resilience may be part genetic in a 'survive or die' mode from a base-set of inherent information each species is born with, but it can be studied and understood.

We can do this through self-study. Start by taking a look at what was going on that helped us get through things. We can dissect those situations. We may recognize we were born with a certain resilience and, beyond that, a level of positive thinking that got us through something. By studying what we are skilled at and what we need to learn, we can help ourselves prepare for future crises, or alleviate them.

Prevention includes: Positive thinking, gratitude, being actively involved in understanding our 'self'—looking at our patterns can prevent us from getting mixed up in negative stuff later on.

This doesn't mean thinking everything is rosy all the time, it means being solution oriented, having a team or tribe to rely on, knowing how to do things by ourself because we have previously asked for help, taken the time to learn, and by helping others which then expanded our skillset. When we have resilient qualities, we rebound from setbacks quicker than if we're not resilient. We can completely steer away from getting mired in the sticky mud of negative situations.

Resilience doesn't make problems go away, but it allows a person to see past problems, see a way through them, and to handle them with less stress than a non-resilient person might. The more resilient a person is, the more foresight they have to switch gears and change things up when recognizing there are potential issues.

It is about recognizing your strengths of having dealt with those situations and building more strength to continue along a healthy road.

So, what adds to that strength we were born with?

Connection. Solid relationships with trust. Finding them. Building them.

Especially with yourself. I needed a solid relationship with myself and to believe in myself in order to let go of some of those friendships that weren't friendships. They offered a sense of belonging because I needed to feel wanted. But they weren't' healthy. I was young and I didn't understand that. But even when I was older, I still fell into a few traps. I wanted validation so I put up with poor treatment. Less than honorable friendships.

So, yes, connection with the self first, and then others. It helps, though, if you do have a mentor because then that mentor can help you appreciate and get in touch with your own feelings and values. We can sum that up by saying connection with the higher self is absolutely one way to power up.

Another resilience builder is gratitude: making each day meaningful and meaning full by appreciating all that is around. Some might say gratitude is overrated or everybody's talking about gratitude journals and acts of kindness. Don't knock it until you try it—that's what I say. It totally changes one's perspective. There's a caveat though. Gratitude only works when it's practiced from an authentic place and not with expectations. Paying something forward is great, but if a person does it only to talk about it to everyone and get the pats on the back for being so wonderful, then maybe it's not paying it forward but self-aggrandizing.

We've come to that word 'authenticity'. It's as overused as it is misunderstood. Keep this in mind. It simply means being true to your core values.

Resilience is built through self care—another trending word. What it means is caring for the self in all areas from physical care, like getting enough sleep, and I know I've messed up on that in the past, to eating healthy food (guilty of not), to emotional self care and the protection of mental health which is fueled by the people you hang out with and the activities you participate in.

Be careful not to misunderstand self care. It does not mean beating yourself up if you eat chips. The worst thing that can happen with the self care thing is to buy into every statement in social media so that if you even look at a cookie you are to feel shame. What you think is who you are. What you do next determines who you are too. If what you do next is think you are a loser, then that is not good. Self care needs to be explained with a level of joy and happiness at the core teachings. Self care is not a harsh diet and a grueling work out if you're going to feel bad about not dieting or working out well enough. It's a really destructive cycle in that case.

Self care is different for everyone. If you managed to have a shower when you didn't think you could, then that is self care. If you stayed in bed because you were having a bad day, then that is self care as long as you knew that you deserved it and that if it becomes a pattern you will ask for professional help. Self care is not telling yourself you are lazy, worthless, or a waste of time. It's doing all the things that make you feel the opposite of those things. And it is understanding what you want for yourself so that you are facing—no matter how active or inactive you are on any given day—in the direction of your dreams. Hmmm, In The Direction Of Your Dreams. Now there's a book title.

Experiences On Call

India Juliet Kilo Lima

HEAD-ON-COLLISION-FOUR-MILES-
EAST-SPRUCE-ON-ROUTE-NINE.

I'd closed the door to my house in the City of Mahnomen, duty bag and snacks in one hand. Once in the squad car, at the same time as I caught Brook Lynn waving to me from the front room's window, dispatch reported the collision that was out in a rural area.

Overhead lights and siren, my speed increased to eighty-miles-an-hour when I was out of town. Cars pulled over to the shoulder as I whizzed by, slowed to turn east onto a county road, then punched the pedal to the metal again. Ten minutes later I arrived on scene.

An old, but well-maintained farm truck lay in the westbound ditch. Another vehicle blocked northbound traffic as it was only partially in the ditch. An older man was walking through the tall weeds. It turned out he was trying to get around the car to reach his wife on the passenger side.

I exited my squad car and ran toward the man who had opened the door; a woman was struggling to get out. Moments later, I could see that her feet were broken, but she managed to get out and began walking around, in the ditch, dazed and confused.

I got her to sit just as the ambulance showed. Meanwhile, her husband was pacing.

I then ran to the other vehicle blocking northbound traffic. The driver was in bad shape. I dashed to the passenger side and opened the door to deal with the passenger: no response, no movement, no rising and falling of his chest. No pulse. He was no longer with us.

I was simultaneously radioing dispatch to send the life flight to the field right next to our location—the driver was barely hanging on.

CONFIRMED-LIFE-FLIGHT-IS-SCRAM-BLING-COPY-TEN-FOUR

By this time there were two ambulances on scene. One was tending to the woman with two broken feet. The other paramedics were closer to me, dealing with the passenger that I'd just called a life flight for.

Suddenly, the pacing husband of the woman whose feet were broken collapsed. One of the paramedics and I ran to where he'd fallen. He was unresponsive and not breathing; I began performing CPR while the paramedic ran for a gurney.

ETA-LIFE-FLIGHT-TWO-MINUTES-COPY-TEN-FOUR

We were two teams hard at work—one on the male who was barely hanging on, and one trying to revive the older male whose wife was already in an ambulance. Paramedics took over with the downed male, and I returned to the barely-hanging-on male, helping to get the gurney he was on through the weeds in the ditch, and into the field.

The whirring chopper blades kicked up a wind over me, and the machine set down. We pushed the gurney under the blades and to the door. It seemed the chopper took off the instant the patient was loaded.

I raced back to the scene, hopping over rocks, ruts, and wading through the weeds. The older man who had collapsed was pronounced dead by the paramedics. It was later discovered he'd suffered a torn aorta that ultimately took his life on the scene.

And then family arrived at the scene and were told the news of their father, and that their mother had already been ambulanced to the hospital.

I was heartbroken—and shocked—that a husband, bravely tending to his injured wife, then moving around the crash scene, had just died. He'd seemed fine a few minutes before. He'd been walking and talking. He'd been alive, albeit operating on shock and adrenaline.

It was hard to fully identify my feelings. I was on scene, and sad that his wife would be at the hospital having her injuries treated, not knowing, back at the scene, her husband had died. A massive sense of compassion and duty overwhelmed me. I didn't want this dead husband, whose family had arrived and needed to be with their mother, to be alone.

I respectfully asked the family on scene if I could accompany their father on his journey to the location his body would have to be transported to—in this case it was a funeral home. They gave their blessing and headed to the hospital to their mother.

INVESTIGATION-AND-TOW-TRUCKS-ENROUTE-COPY-TEN-FOUR

Addendum:

FUNERAL PARLOR

Police officers are not just all lights and sirens. They are compassionate. They are interested in the lives of others. Their involvement stretches beyond the limits of what the average person may think happens behind the scenes.

The sheriff approved my request to accompany the man's body who had just died of a heart attack at the scene.

I pulled my squad car in as the funeral home director was opening the garage door to the facility. I walked up to the gurney and touched the man's arm and said, "I am here with you."

We pushed the gurney into the prep room where I was not only a companion for the dead, but a student, receiving a lesson on how bodies are prepared for preservation. A time to meet my sense of empathy and an opportunity to learn.

This is the night that I learned the time we spend caring for someone does not end with death.

I stayed through the embalming and learned about the process.

I witnessed the caring ways the staff at the funeral home take care of our loved ones and ensure every post-life moment is dignified.

I left the funeral home hours later feeling good about my decision to be with this man during this time. But I also felt panic and confusion. I began thinking about my own death. The thoughts of my status as a single parent, and how my daughter would be left alone, made me uncomfortable. I though about how much she would miss me; I thought about how much loss she would feel.

Over time, I was able to realize that it is vital for our life-experience to go through things others might say are weird, or some might tell you are unnecessary. Every opportunity to learn about our fear of death is a massive invitation to work through our feelings. Knowledge is golden, but it is the processing of thoughts because of that knowledge that creates the value.

Mike November Oscar Papa

The dreaded five-in-the-morning dispatch call. There are three reasons why these calls are dreaded. First, no one wants to find someone's deceased relatives; second, no one wants to find a deceased relative after two weeks; three, no one wants to work a death investigation two hours before their shift is about to end. This call is a recipe for working until noon rather then seven a.m.

Though there is no certain time for death because death can come at any time, hospital staff and emergency personnel share that the majority of deaths come between three and five in the morning. Or at least reports of them do. In reaching out to numerous first responders, they say that the bell tolls at these hours because this is the time that a body begins to prepare for the day's activity—it has to do with circadian rhythm. Others believe the body is the weakest in those hours—medical staff have told me adrenaline and anti-inflammatory hormones are the lowest at that time, and that causes airways to narrow—and that spasm-triggering compounds are higher at that time of day.

As for reports of death, well, early morning is a time when people stir in the early morning hours and wake and find their loved ones deceased.

The well-being check that will always stick with me was a hot July day. The sun had been blasting the earth at a steady 80 degrees for a few weeks now and even at five in the morning it was warm.

A family member who lived out of state had called the sheriff's office to report he hadn't heard from his father in approximately two weeks. The son stated he normally heard from his father every couple days—could someone check?

I was alone in my vehicle and headed out to the country. A few miles east into the county sat a house-trailer at the end of a short, gravel driveway. Parked outside the house was an old truck. The grass in the yard was long and weeds had taken over the entire space.

The curtains in the house were open.

As I peeked through the windows, I could see the television was on but there was no other movement to indicate someone was up and around... or at home.

I walked around the outside of the trailer and noticed there was no air conditioner running. It was when I approached the back side of the trailer that my nose recognized the distinct sickly-sweet odor.

Contrary to what a person might think, it's not the smell of decaying animals. It's chemicals emitted into the air mixed with sour garbage juices at the bottom of a dumpster—got that? Then go further and mix it with decaying fish and vomit.

The static of the television was audible and, as I looked closer, there appeared hundreds of flies plastered to the glass window trying to find an escape. It was like a black curtain over the back window.

This is when I knew that there was someone, not something, deceased inside. I informed dispatch of what I was seeing and smelling and waited for another officer to arrive. We knocked on the door, then the windows—just in case someone was inside—then kicked in that same front door.

WOOOOOOOOFFFFF! Gag reflexes kicked in instantly. Both of us had to back away and let the smell dissipate somewhat. At the least, we hoped it would make our next attempt easier.

Equipped with Vicks vapor rub, we pushed the gel into our noses then donned blue face masks.

As we entered the second time, an emaciated, black, mixed breed dog came running out of the residence and took off into the trees surrounding the trailer.

We began to make our way through the rooms, starting in the living room and moving to the kitchen. Even through the Vicks and mask the odor was sickening. We proceeded to the bedrooms. As we approached the master bedroom my stomach turned as if I had the flu. I was doing everything to take shallow breaths due to the overwhelming odor consuming my airways, causing vomit to enter the back of my throat.

The door to the master bedroom was open; the chemical smell of decay worsened with every step toward the room.

A man's body lay on the ground. What with the temperature being over eighty for a long time, the body had bloated to twice the size of a human. His limbs appeared to have been partially eaten by his dog. The maggots and flies were as thick as if in a queen bee's nest.

As I held my hand over my mouth, I ran as fast as I could through the narrow hallway, through the kitchen, out onto the front steps and began to vomit. I couldn't stop vomiting as the odor was hanging outside still; every time I took a breath, I could only smell decaying body.

My colleague came out shortly after me. In true cop humor he laughed and made a joke. "Hmmm, you had spaghetti for dinner. Nice."

I had no strength to reply.

He relayed to dispatch that we needed the funeral home personnel to our location.

Half an hour later, they showed up and found us standing near the road. It was the closest I could get to the house without being triggered by the smell.

The funeral home director was briefed on what we had found. He suggested we come in and help with removing the body. This is the last thing I wanted to do; I did not want to go back in there with that smell, the body, the maggots, and flies. However, it was my job and I had to muster up the courage and choke down the vomit.

The funeral director explained that he would go in and take pics and samples of the insects then call us to come in when he was finished.

Thank goodness he was considerate in limiting our time in the house. He did explain that when we went to move the body we had to do so in a certain way—instead of lifting the body we would have to try to slide the body bag under the man, then slowly move him onto it. The risk of him popping—as in exploding—and all the fluids and gasses going everywhere were highly probable. If we could get him into the bag before it happened, it would be better for everyone.

I summoned the strength—determination served me—and put on a new layer of Vicks then donned a new mask. The Vicks was so thick my eyes were watering. Rubber clothes and boot coverings were a must.

When we entered the house, we moved with purpose; there was no diddle-daddling around. Straight to the room and, under instruction from the funeral director, we got into position. My heart was thumping out of my chest, sweat beaded and then dripped off my forehead, my uniform under the protective clothing was stuck to me from sweat. I batted off flies like a crazy person, then knelt at the body's feet—or where the feet once were.

We slid the bag inch by inch until it was far enough under that we could move the body with less risk than before. Then the funeral worker pushed the body a little, but that was it. It was a little push too much. It was as if the body had been shaken up like a can full of cola. The body exploded. Fluids began to run out onto my boot coverings and also onto the funeral staff and the other officer. At this point it was a matter of getting it in the bag quickly. As they were zipping up the body bag I ran through the trailer as fast as I could, then vomited in the front yard.

A short time later, they exited with the deceased in the body bag and placed him into the back of their car to be taken to the funeral home.

Connection is everything. My heart often went out to those who had passed alone or passed and no one had known—they hadn't had a buddy system, or a buddy. Every call I went on that echoed loneliness took a piece of me—we need each other; we are a sociable species.

Let's Coach

Teresa, I often feel ambushed by my family members who have no problem holding back their opinions on how I should live my life. How do I make this stop?

Can I just say opinions are like assholes? Everyone has one, and move along now. When other people want to give advice and opinions, ask yourself this question: what are their intentions and motivations... where are they coming from?

A common perception people have is that they think everyone has the same 'value' as they have. It's common but naïve to assume that 'someone' has the same qualities as yourself, or prioritizes in the same way. Many a disappointment or disagreement has been caused by thinking this way. What is important to you is not necessarily important to someone else.

Many people believe that they want in life is what other people want in life. Whether positive or negative, the process of projecting beliefs only creates bigger issues.

I like to look at all relationships based on reliability and truth. First things first: when someone is projecting their beliefs, ask yourself if the person is an expert or an authority in the area they are speaking about. For instance, when looking for advice to start a new career, you aren't going listen to someone who hasn't worked a day in their life. Or if you are looking for advice on how to be in a strong, healthy, long-lasting relationship you sure aren't going to take the advice from someone who has been divorced three times and is a daily complainer about their current relationship. The best place to get advice is from someone who has done what you are trying to do. Those other people don't have the competence to advise you properly.

Consult an expert… that is step one. Step two is to ask if the person who is sharing their opinions cares about you. Do they have your best interest at heart, do they value where you are going, do they want to invest in your growth?

The step three question is to ask yourself if the person practices what they preach. Finally… check in with yourself to remind yourself that you didn't solicit the information. You asked how to make it stop. Well, you are the only one who can make it stop.

A simple statement that fits your relationship and style with them should be enough to stop them. If they do not stop, then it would be wise to evaluate the reasons you keep engaging with the 'opinion offerer'.

Some people might find this works: "Hey, dude. I get that you have a lot to say, but right now I'm working this one out on my own."

Others may want to go further in terms of sharing that you're going through some changes in the way you live and thrive, therefore some of the old ways of 'the relationship' are not going to work at this time.

When someone doesn't let up and prevents positivity, then that's often the time to walk away. That walking away is the lesson 'we' needed as well as perhaps what they needed. We get to choose our life-classroom experiences when we're in those learning spaces.

When we make massive efforts to be everything to someone, even to everyone, then we stop being 'all' to ourselves. This is a sign we're off balance—that our relationship or relationships are not the healthiest. When someone tries to be 'everything' to you and for you, then that is also a sign they're not living their best lives.

We need to be carers of ourselves. That is the best example we can give to others. Whether they learn from their example is not 'our' business.

Let's Coach

Teresa, How the hell does a person make a fresh start? A complete do-over? I mean financial, emotional, everything. You see... I'm coming from this angle: I want to leave a relationship that is flat. There's no horrible abuse, I just am tired of going through the motions, and I have this idea— no, I might as well say it: it's my dream. I want total simplicity. Right now, I feel that the house is cluttered, I have lots of bills, I am working every weekday and just crashing on the weekend until Monday rolls around again. Barely living paycheck to paycheck. My husband is the same. He does the same. Doesn't say anything about it. This is not the life I signed up for. People say they feel like running away to a desert island, but they don't do it. I am feeling like I have to do that in order to gain my sanity. Where do I start? I feel there's more for me, but I don't know what.

Wow, that's quite the list. And let me congratulate you on being able to put it all down in one collective observation.

I want you to start by knowing that you are being heard— there's a lot of courage in sharing all that.

Funny you should mention running way to a desert island because an island is a tool you can use to get moving. Wait, don't pack your bags—you're not going on an all expense paid trip to an island. Running away never solves anything… well, maybe if you're being chased by a bear. Running toward is better. But first you have to figure out where you're at in a less frantic way.

So, about that island.

I want you to imagine you are on an island. Let's call it Island A. On island A is everything that is currently going on. All the things that you talked about in your question. Mondays are just a continuation of frantic Friday, and the weekends are never remembered because you've crashed through them.

In the distance, there is another island. Island B. Island B is a place you know about and have dreamed about. Your heart tells you every day you want to live on Island B. The problem is, you don't know how to get to Island B.

When you contact the specialist who is the expert on getting to Island B you learn that the first requirement of getting there is for travelers to become aware of what works on Island A and what doesn't work on Island A.

When the list is complete, the expert shows the traveler how to throw what's not working into the ocean. There is a different way for each 'thing' because of the heaviness of that thing, and the weather conditions—wind—at the time they get rid of those things.

The next stage is to step into the ocean and begin swimming. The expert will have the travelers swim through all those 'things' that are floating in the ocean. If the traveler doesn't know how to swim, the expert will teach them.

All through the swim, the expert is in a little boat, cheering on the traveler who is swimming past, around, and through the stuff that was thrown in.

My point is, we can only get to where we want to be by understanding where we are, what we want to get rid of, why we want to, and how we can remove those things from our lives.

We do so by looking inside the self—for those answers are within each person, each traveler. And those travel experts, of which I am one, can help you do that.

Let's Coach

Please don't tell me to forgive someone... I can't. I won't. But my anger is sucking all the energy from me. Friends are drifting... one said I am always talking about how my ex hurt me. How do I not let this take over?

When a person is focused on negatives from the past, they struggle to build their future. You already know that because you have had the courage to ask the question, and you recognize that your friends are drifting. You've even listened to at least one friend by saying they've noticed how you're always talking about your ex.

I'd like you to think of forgiveness as a process—rather than think it is something you 'have' or 'don't have'. Forgiveness is a process you choose to work through.

There is self forgiveness and there is the forgiving of others. Forgiveness brings a kind of freedom that allows a person to flourish.

Some people think forgiveness is conditional, meaning the person who perceives they are harmed will forgive if the 'offender' apologizes, compromises, or accepts responsibility. The thing is, in life, we are responsible for ourselves. Other people's inner-goings-on are their business. A conditional forgiveness does not reach the root because there is always a bit of a 'checking on the other person who wronged you'.

Forgiveness is something you do for yourself. Sure, it may positively affect the other person or group who you believe wronged or hurt you, but that is not the purpose of forgiveness. Forgiveness is an inside job for inside results.

The process of forgiveness begins with our understanding of how we perceive our world and the things that happen to us. When we are able to work through the process completely, we will find that true forgiveness is unconditional—it is done with no expectations that we will receive something externally in return for the forgiveness we give. This is difficult because it is human nature to expect something in return for an action. We're just not used to going inside and seeing we can give to ourselves and, ultimately, receive from ourselves the gift of inner peace.

Forgiveness is a kind of letting go. I had to do this with my brother who betrayed me years ago. When I let go, through a process of understanding that my ongoing choice to keep being angry was nothing to do with him, the peace rolled in. It didn't mean I had to forget. In fact, remembering in a healthy way allows me to navigate my way through new relationships, it meant I had nothing to do with his initial actions, and every-thing to do with how I responded to them.

Once again, we become unmesswithable through a process of self love and self knowledge.

It is possible that you can let go of the hurt you feel for your ex. To not let go is holding yourself back from your true poten-tial to love yourself wholly. Not letting go—continuing to speak about the anger—is a sign that there are more lessons for you. None of this has anything to do with your ex.

Okay, I know you might be 'but, but, but, Teresa, you don't get how bad it was… he did this and he's still doing that, and I lost the house because of him, and the kids are…. and I'll never trust…' That's okay, you're still in the lesson.

We do not have to give our power to others. That is what we do when we react and create drama, even when the offense is blatantly abusive, against the law, and horrific. We can still choose to respond in a way that serves us 'forward'.

You've probably heard, people come into our lives sometimes for a season, reason, or a lifetime. Determining which it is can help with forgiveness. The people who hurt others the most are likely in the season and reason category.

Always remember, just because someone is part of your family does not mean you have to allow them into your life to cause you pain. It is important to recognize that people who have hurt you came into your life for a reason—you are in a class-room (we all are) learning how to care for ourselves and reach our highest potential… that includes learning to navigate the dynamics of relationships.

Let's Coach

Discipline is a word that scares people. They hear it and back away. Let's get it out of the way up front. Discipline, and staying power (aka consistency), comes from within and represent systematic and progressive processes.

When we call something a process, it is easier to, well, process. We get the idea there are stages to achieving something. It gets better when we say those stages can be taken with baby steps. Even better when we say there's more success when we approach change by taking baby steps.

To start fresh and stay energized a person cannot tackle everything at once nor make whole life changes at the same time. We humans are silly people, and we get these grand ideas then start out toward a goal with great enthusiasm and add all kinds of 'have to do this and that' to the enthusiasm. A ton of 'doing this and that' is not sustainable. We wake up the morning after a decision and think that we can achieve something as if we have 'developed' new habits in our sleep.

We don't develop ten new habits or even one overnight. That is impossible. Instead of tackling everything at once we need to break things down until you find the first, small, actionable steps. Oh, but we want it all, right now: the new job, apartment, the separation, the weight loss—after all, you have been through hell already. We've seen so many ads on social media with fresh-faced individuals who are living the life. They have it, we say, so I can have it too. Look! The banner on the ad says all these people have the life they dreamed of.

Read the small print in that contract you signed for life. Becoming a master carpenter, plumber, bricklayer takes time. That's why there are apprenticeships. Life is the same. We need to start by unraveling what is the most important thing and WHY that is important and ripe for change.

It doesn't mean that, while you are learning, and while you are establishing habits. life cannot be fun, and change won't show up along the way. The whole journey is more than the destination.

Starting fresh means starting at the first step to a staircase, which is identifying where you want to be. Your goal. The first thing to do is ask yourself WHY. If your WHY isn't big enough, moving enough, meaningful enough to you, the outcome will not be reached or sustained. Then you climb to the next step which would be to list the benefits of achieving the goal. Lift your foot to the next step which might be to list the obstacles that are preventing you from getting to your goal. Then climb a little higher on the staircase and list the knowledge and skills you need to succeed and who and what can help you reach the goal.

Develop a plan of action. Slowly and systemically climb a metaphoric staircase.

I've written about how I climbed this staircase. I even talked about how I slipped down a few stairs and got back up. I talked about each step I took to get to the point in my life where I am now sharing my thoughts with others who want to listen. The plan of action is the most critical part as it forms the foundation of all your efforts. The more thorough the plan, the better the outcome, and you need to fully embrace your WHY- your WHY has to align.

Part Three: Determination

Hyena

Something we were withholding made us weak
Until we found out that it was ourselves.
—Robert Frost

We were going to Alaska. She didn't know it yet, but I was excited. I pictured travel posters: 'See the world'. It was ironic that Alaska's motto was North to the Future.

I knew so much about her potential and her future. She knew she needed to make the change and leave Minnesota. She wanted to learn more—she couldn't learn more where she was. Alaska was the perfect opportunity.

Of course, just as I knew about Alaska, there were other seeds being planted by me, and other energies out there. She had to come to the decisions she did, especially after the life-changing call where her partner-colleague, Chris Dewey, was killed. And she did.

She also knew there were limitations for her—sadly, as a female—in a male dominated profession, especially in the mid-west. We weren't exactly in NYC or LA, though the gender divide is a national one with no department unaffected.

I managed to catch her attention when I howled when she made the decision to apply to Alaska. And then again when she got the position. I know because she tipped her head and looked over to

255

where I was racing around the rocking chair. I hoped we'd connect in person-to-guide, soon.

She'd done so well in Minnesota; she needed more. More responsibility, more respect, more life. We were getting closer to fully understanding each other and closer to her future which I saw, and she did not—I had no idea how I would share with her what that would look like, but I let that go.

She'd had so much experience in the rural areas on account of her being who she was—dedicated and not afraid to step in—and because officers there who had her initiative could take on tasks that ordinarily, in a department-by-department police station of a big city, would have been passed to specialists and micromanaged.

I longed to speak to her about some of her calls. I wanted to discuss with her how the future might look in five and then ten years... that it might not be policing at all, but a larger role in helping others. But we hadn't crossed that bridge yet.

And I wanted to tell her how proud I was about the way she approached her life. She'd pulled herself into understanding the dangers of the job and, while she was always keenly aware of those dangers, her duty to serve was strong. Yet it wasn't stronger than her love for Brook Lynn. That was a different kind of love. She was simply driven to serve and succeed in her career. Alaska would do that for her.

Sometimes, in the mornings, when I thought she sensed me more than ever, I started to say good morning right after she'd hit the snooze button, when her eyes were still closed. Sometimes she'd open her eyes and look around the room. I was close. I persevered.

And then, one day, we all got on a plane to Anchorage. Me, under the seat in front of her, avoiding being stepped on by her size 8s... swirling around and curling up so that I could watch our future pan out in her eyes.

North, to Alaska

In the 2011-2012 season, Anchorage, Alaska received a record breaking 133.6 inches of snow. This broke the previous record of 132.6 inches. So why would a police officer who was a single mom want to go, from the freezing temperatures of Minnesota, 3000 miles northwest to such a place? Punishment or professional development? I opted to treat it as the second. I learned so much there. That's where I became a detective.

The police department in Anchorage served a population over 250,000. This was quite different than the Midwest—Detroit Lakes 5000, Mahnomen county 10,000, and even Fargo's 100,000.

I started on night shift, then I began to train as a detective. Most officers need a year before they write the exam. I received approval to write it at six months and sailed through. After officially passing my department's exam and interview phase—I scored the highest of any of the officers writing the exam at that time—I was hired as their detective and was sent to Las Vegas for formal training.

There are advantages to rural locations, like Detroit Lakes, such as having to multitask due to the lack of specialities being just down the hall. I'd picked up a lot of knowledge, and my love of learning and good study habits helped too.

Brook Lynn and I moved to a residence just doors away from the police station—on the same street. She was able to stay home when I was working, and go to school.

The first part of Alaska was more training than work—extensive training. The calls when I worked as a detective were a lot of sexual assaults. I worked on a financial investigation involving embezzlement. The investigation resulted in the recovery of a large amount of money and cache of materials. The tracking work alone resulted in my office being piled with the paper from a paper trail—receipts and purchase orders. and tracking all over the country, culminating in me personally kicking in a door to the perpetrator's Anchorage residence.

The wild thing about this investigation, aside from the massive paper trail and extensive tracking, was the nature of the crime. It had started with a university employee funding her passion of anime with some equipment that she used for personal use. She then—it seemed—became addicted to spending the university's money on an excess of items for herself via the internet. Some things she had delivered to the university and other items to her home. When we conducted the raid, her garage was filled with items piled to the ceiling.

Her crime did not injure anyone, in the way that the shooting of Chris Dewey caused irreparable damage, but it destroyed trust. The costs trickled down to all those who supported the university through enrollment fees.

The investigation was complicated, and the mental capacity to understand why such a crime would be perpetrated even more complex.

Addiction is not only a disease that is related to drugs or alcohol, sex, or gambling. It can come in terms of hoarding, wanting, obtaining, and gaining 'things', then become so strong that a person finds illicit ways to support the purchasing of goods.

I worked hard in Anchorage. I felt pulled back to Minnesota because of my roots. Besides, I was at my peak.

Funny how that works. We go through life's trials, repeat lessons, suffer along the way in various ways, and then one day we realize it was all for a reason. Suddenly, we find ourselves liking who we see in the mirror. We are ready to acknowledge all we have become.

Cold Rooms and Change

In the Midwest, on the front lines, I'd become an expert at working a crime scene, mass casualty event, or a disturbance. I'd worked the active hours—nightshifts. I knew all the steps to take, what to watch for, how to protect myself and my fellow officers. I knew what goes in must come out of all scenes. Alaska gave me the opportunity to learn about the back-end. I had to shift my brain and learn to work with what other officers brought me. I had to trust they were trained to walk through those scenes alone and produce a good case into which I could dive and obtain a conviction.

No longer a road officer, I filled the role of detective. The challenge was what I needed. I was able to up my game and teach others how to wrap up a crime scene so that it could be delivered to me with a little red bow around it. Together, as a team, the goal was to be error-free, or make as few mistakes as possible.

I started where I had the most experience—sexual assault cases. I began to learn about the appropriate steps in investigating a sexual assault case in order to bring it to court.

I had worked in 'cop mode' for a long time, and my brain tended to stay there: focus on the case, make the arrest, get the win. But, with sexual assaults, I had to engage more empathy. This pivot was necessary on so many levels. Women and men who have been violated—yes, men can be assaulted too—suffer a great deal, including that their dignity has been taken from them. When they report this to the police, or have to repeat their story over to various law enforcement officers, they can feel ashamed, less than, and even embarrassed. Making the shift to be with the victim in real time, at the moment they begin speaking, is a skill, and I needed to hone that skill. Case after case, as I responded to sexual assault calls, I realized the victim was traumatized over and over. This re-traumatization was brutal on the victims and only served to negatively affect their healing. I began to see that the system, as a whole, was broken. Not just in my department but country wide. In most instances, the victim (survivor) would show up to the emergency room, tell the emergency staff what had happened, go through extensive questioning—which meant answering personal questions that involved the most intimate part of their lives—and then, in a somewhat 'degraded' state, they'd have a sexual assault evaluation performed on them consisting of swabbing for DNA in intimate areas, having pictures of their bodies taken, holding out their hands to have their finger nails trimmed, experience the scrapes or swipes of swabs along their skin where they were bitten, licked, or 'kissed'. Hours and hours of this only to have to repeat the verbal part of it again to a police officer who was dispatched to take the report.

Imagine going through this for hours, then having to repeat it again to an officer—quite often a male officer if you are female, or a female officer if you are a male, only to have the officer catch something in the story that requires the victim to have to have more swabs, samples, and photos taken—which means getting undressed again. And... when that is over, to be sent on their way with no resources, no help, and their attacker still out there.

The fear a survivor holds, wondering if the suspect will come back for them, is huge—even when that perpetrator is caught... sometimes, especially then. Then there is the loneliness and the shame as the victim-survivor relives the event and experiences how 'alone' they were in the assault. After that, the hurt kicks in and the stories begin—the stories men and women survivors begin telling themselves—they involve second guessing themselves, frustrating, as they perceive they put themselves in the position of vulnerability, or stories that involve old wounds or bring about newfound memories of a previous assault or similar situation they hadn't even consciously known they'd experienced. Something about their 'lifestyle' will begin to get twisted by their imagination and will morph even more because of the way the system operates. They may come to feel that the perpetrator has more rights than they do.

It doesn't stop there—but it certainly can when a victim just withdraws their complaint because it is overwhelmingly painful (though some laws in some places exist to prosecute regardless of a victim's cooperation). When a suspect is arrested, the victim has to go to court and look the person in the eyes and, AGAIN, tell their story in front of an audience, and the person who did this to them. This is then the continuation of reliving the trauma, thus retraumatizing them.

I couldn't stand how we were revictimizing survivors. It needed to change. I needed to learn to pivot and shift. I needed to learn to be more present. This is where Sexual Assault Training came in, and then began the creation of a Sexual Assault Response Team (SART) in our area.

I asked, and I received, thanks to my lieutenant and police chief, who were beacons of light. They supported my proactivity, and my goal for me and my fellow officers to be better. A short time after I made my request—that we needed change in our department in the way we handled sexual assaults - I was flown to Texas for a two-week training in Sexual Assault Response Teams.

SART – Sexual Assault Response Teams are a partnerships of agencies that serve sexual assault victims. It's a true alliance whereby myriad groups come together: victim advocates, police, doctors, medical examiners, scientists, prosecuting lawyers and defending council too. Professionals work together to create guidelines that put victims' needs first, make offenders accountable, and keep public safety as the overall goal. We were made aware of the whys of needing to be better for our victims and communities as a whole, and then shown how we could do that. The main driver of this was that, without us coming together, nothing could be changed. I completed the training with absolute confidence I could bring the message back to Alaska. I returned, invigorated, ready to make change, wanting to make change.

This is what I did.

Back in my community we rallied—Chiefs of Police, Officers, hospital CEOs, victim advocacy groups, judges, prosecutors, and defense attorneys along with many other professions and individuals within those professions. The focus was to help sexual assault service providers come together to build and then maintain strong professional group responses to sexual violence. We were committed to victims' rights and needs, and organized ourselves to make evidence collection a more humane experience, and to teach those in the community about the services relating to prevention and intervention. We all came together to streamline for the survivors and make the process of reporting sexual violence less scary and shameful.

We created a system. As the detective and advocate, I was on the front line of that system; leading by taking what I'd learned in Texas and implementing it in my department. I began educating officers on sexual violence, and explaining how we were going to make a change on how we were going to work together with numerous community agencies. We worked together and we worked hard. Through it all we created a system where survivors no longer had to share their story multiple times. Leading this part of the team for my agency was incredibly rewarding. I had a lot of pride in working with a great community and seeing that we made a difference. Most importantly, through this coalition, we were able to hold offenders accountable for their actions (my detective hat just went back on).

I didn't stop there. The initiative created a little fire within me. I requested to be sent to Tampa, Florida—yes, Alaska to TX then to FL—for more training. While I felt it was a big ask, I wanted to be considered in taking a Rape Aggression Defense training. I explained why it was important, and what it would bring back to my department as a whole. Three months later, I touched down in Tampa.

Rape Aggression Defense System (RAD) is a program which addresses 'real' and 'doable' self defense. It teaches tactics and techniques in a thorough way so that women can understand—through being aware—of what assault is, and then learn about prevention, how to reduce their risks of becoming a victim, avoidance, and focus on the basics of hands-on defense training. RAD instruction contains learnable, effective, and proven self-defence strategies. RAD gives women the confidence and solid information so that they can make smart decisions on how to protect themselves.

This training was important to me to bring to Alaska because the state had many colleges and military bases in the area which statistically placed people at a higher risk. After the training, I began to think about my teenage daughter, and applied my energy of bringing the program to the community through my concern for her. I wanted to make sure all women were able to protect themselves, including my daughter.

This is what I did: I brought that training back to my department and began holding classes three times a week. I taught many women how to protect themselves. The work I was doing in RAD caught the eye of our local air force base leaders. I was pulled into the Chief's office one day—which can be nerve wracking for fear of being in trouble. When I closed the door, the Chief said, "I got a call from a commander at the air force base." My mind immediately went south—what did I do? Is my child okay? I had family in the military—had someone died?

The Chief continued to explain that the commander on the base had noticed my movement with RAD and requested I come to teach the females there. My Chief told me he would approve it if I was up to the challenge. Of course I was. I rounded up a team of instructors and introduced RAD to the United States Airforce. The response from the women and commanders who participated was phenomenal. It was held in such high regard that, after training, I worked with the Commander to send air force women to RAD training so they could start teaching it themselves.

New Challenges Alaska

With SART and RAD in full swing, I was now up for another challenge or learning experience. At this time mental health awareness was coming full steam ahead. I'd responded—as a detective—to multiple calls of service for suicide attempts, substance abuse (such as drug overdoses, alcoholism), homeless person incidents, and many other categories of crisis. My fellow officers and I didn't always know how best to respond to mental health issues. At that time, the only thing we could do was arrest the individual for the most minor crime to get them off the street, out of their house, and away from the public—basically remove them from the people who felt uncomfortable having them around. How was this beneficial to them? And how was it beneficial to law enforcement and the criminal justice system?

One thing I learned is, if you don't ask, the answer will always be the same as no. I had to ask again. This time, with my hands behind my back swaying back and forth with a grin on my face, I asked the chief and lieutenant if it would be possible to send me to Crisis Intervention Training (CIT). I explained that I wanted for our department to be able to respond to mental health illnesses in a different manner than we had been—arresting them.

I pulled the hat trick. Three for three. I was able to attend CIT training for a week in Anchorage, Alaska through National Alliance of Mental Illnesses (NAMI)

The average police officer—which is most—is not a trained mental health professional. Their tactics are all about handling criminal activity. Police are not healthcare workers—they are law enforcement officers.

The gap between mental health needs and availability of services—country-wide—is huge. The general public and even family often find themselves unable to handle situations that involved mental health crises. One example of many involves an incident in 2020 where a navy veteran experienced paranoia. His family called on the police to help. Sadly, the veteran died as a result of the restraint that the police officer used when he responded to the crisis.

We are all witnesses to the events around us that involve mental health crises. Trusted reporters and media informs us that incidents involving mental health issues are increasing as the number of those diagnosed and undiagnosed with mental health conditions find their way into dangerous situations in which the police are ultimately involved.

Crisis Intervention Teams (CIT) are about bringing mental health service providers, with front line emergency medical services, together with other advocates, law enforcement, and community leaders. The idea is to have a collective expertise so that when the front-line personnel are the police—due to dangerous conditions involving weapons or threats—there is an adjusted response that takes into consideration the mental health. But greater than that, the team initiative is to prevent these incidents from happening, from having law enforcement involved. CIT advocates and teaches methodology in dealing with mental health crises by way of de-escalation, and it helps educate those in law enforcement to slow down, listen carefully, and not overreact. Ultimately, those with mental health issues require patience and connection. CIT initiatives allow community to offer just that, a community response to those who find themselves in times of challenge. In this way, jail is not the 'first' or 'go-to' objective.

Alaska was a gold mine for me, for change, for growth, for helping my community and other officers to be better. My experiences in Alaska prepared me to return south with a new perspective and a renewed goal of up-leveling community policing wherever the next part of my career might be.

The Meeting

HYENA

"A voice said, Look me in the stars,"
I started by quoting Robert Frost. I wanted to see if they'd enter
Teresa's mind before she opened her eyes. I almost fell off the bed
when she answered me.

TERESA

"And tell me truly, men of earth."
Was I saying a line of a poem out loud? Was I dreaming? Had
I heard it in my childhood? Maybe I was still sleeping. I was
in my bed in Anchorage, Alaska. Brook Lynn was in her room
down the hall. Check. I'd hit snooze already. Yes. I needed to
open my eyes, get my ass out of bed, and go make a coffee. But
I knew there was another line to that piece. Was it Robert Frost?
I went over what I'd heard in my dream and the line I'd said in
my dream or aloud in my bed.

A voice said, Look me in the stars.

And I had said, tell me truly, men of earth...

HYENA

She'd heard me. So, I spoke the last line.

"If all the soul-and-body scars."

TERESA

"Who said that?" Someone was in my room. Or I was dreaming? Shit. I didn't want to know someone was in my room.

HYENA

"Good morning, sunshine." That's what I led with after the poetry. It was the kind of communication I did within myself, but it came out so she could hear it. She could hear it! She could hear me!

TERESA

I was still in bed. My eyes were still shut. Brook Lynn was in her room. Only two of us lived in this house. Someone was speaking to me from the bottom of the bed. Or I was speaking to myself. Had a just recited poetry? I opened my eyes. A snouty nose poked out of the extra blanket I had near my feet. Had Brook Lynn decided to surprise me with a pet? But the snout was not that of a cat or dog. And those teeth. Plus, it had spoken, hadn't it?

HYENA

"It's kind of a milestone day,"
She could only see my nose. In a flash I wondered if she had her gun at home, and, if it was close, if she'd shoot.

TERESA

"Holy Shit. This can't be real. Okay, real clever. Convincing puppet show, Brook. Enough. This is creepy, not funny."

HYENA

"Not Brook Lynn." (I started to worry.) "Don't panic, Teresa. You know it's not a trick. The only power operating me is a higher one that's, well, fueled by you. Look, this is not the conversation we need to have now, not the whole secrets of the universe thing."

TERESA

"Who?" (I blinked a few more times.) Look, you're freaking me out. Your voice is familiar, and it's coming from my head, not my ears. How's that working?"

HYENA

"I don't make the rules, or choose the timing, so I can't answer that." (I shoved a bit more of my head from the fold on the fleece blanket. In hindsight, it might have been a bit ghost of Christmas future meets a kind of Yogi-Yoda-Hyena.)

TERESA

"What are you doing here?" (I kept my voice low, so Brook Lynn wouldn't wake.)

HYENA

"I've always been here. I mean with you. I don't mean always here under this blanket, or here in Alaska, I mean I've always been with you. But I do like this blanket, and have been sleeping under it, when you sleep, since you got to Alaska.

TERESA

"I'm having a nervous breakdown. That's it. I've lost it. I work hard, overcome all kinds of shit in my childhood, reach my dream of being a police officer, and now I'm a detective—a good detective—and now I've got some kind of brain thing going on. I'm going to close my eyes, open them again, and you'd better be gone."

HYENA

"That's a little dramatic."

TERESA

"Stop it. Just stop. I'm closing my eyes and counting to three. One. Two. Th—"

HYENA

"That's what they say in movies. You know, when a dog comes back as an angel, or a Herbie the Love Bug comes to life—"

TERESA

"I can still hear you. Go away. You're creeping me out. I'm creeping me out."

HYENA

Teresa, this isn't a movie."
This wasn't the way I wanted it to go. "Don't panic. I'm gonna come out. I'll need to shake. Don't scare Brook Lynn when I show myself. When you see I'm not a puppet. You know she doesn't need any stress—remember when she jumped a mile when that frog came through the house when she was five."

I started to drag my whole hyena from under the blanket.

TERESA

"You leave Brook Lynn out of this you pervy little stalker. Hey, how did you know about the frog?"

HYENA

"And by the way, I'm just as surprised as you that you see me today. Listen to me. You know my voice. You've known it since you were born."

TERESA

I must have pulled myself to a sitting position. "This is beyond weird. Tell me something no one would ever know."

HYENA

"Really? We have to go there?"
Maybe there was a mistake, and I did show up early.
"I gotta tell you you're venturing into movie territory again."
By now, half my body was exposed, and I was sitting at the bottom of the bed.
"Fuck, you're stubborn. I can't believe I'm doing this. You know I used to sleep in the crook of your legs in Little Blue."

TERESA

"Hey! No one knows I call it Little Blue. I only ever say that in my head."

HYENA

"No, I called it Little Blue. I named it. Then I gave you that. You're welcome."

TERESA

"Are you saying you're the voice in my head? A concept, but in a form?"

I calmed, grateful that this might not be such a bizarre thing. "So, you're the erm, thing, voice in my head, the feeling that brings out the best in me, the safety net." It felt right saying that.

HYENA

"No shit, Sherlock."
I watched her relax. She even smiled at my joke.
"The word you're looking for is guide. I'm the guide. Your guide."
She relaxed some more so I stood and arched and stretched.

TERESA

"A hyena? Wait a minute. Were you there when Brook Lynn was born? I wrote about a hyena in my journal."

HYENA

"I was there when 'you' were born."

TERESA

"Holy shit." I seemed only able to stick with one phrase of shock. "Why are you in this form? Aren't you supposed to have wings and feathers? Why are you a hyena?"

HYENA

"Because female hyenas are unfuckwithable."

TERESA

"Unfuckwhatable?"

HYENA

"You heard me. Basically: we rule our world."
I let her take that in.

TERESA

All right. You don't have to get in my face with it. I just hadn't heard that before.

HYENA

"It's what you have become. No one messes with you. We could say, for politeness, unmesswithable. Or if they try, you basically say with your actions or body language: 'don't mess with me.' And now it's time to take it to a new level; a new part of your service. You're ready." I finished stretching and let my front legs step forward to get me back into a relaxed laying position. Thought we might as well sleep in a bit. *"It's okay, I'm patient. I'll wait."*

TERESA

"I'm ready?"

HYENA

"You gotta be able to say it without it being a question because you know you're ready for this. This thing we have going here this morning wouldn't have worked if you weren't ready. I'd still be invisible to you. Look, make your coffee, I'm not going anywhere."

TERESA

"I'm gonna do that. I'm gonna go in there and make my coffee and add a spoon of sanity to it. Any luck and you'll be gone when I get back." But deep inside I knew that's not how it would go down. This was real. And I kind of liked the idea of being 'ready' and something magical and more powerful being in my life.

HYENA

"Don't forget… that outlet is touchy. Make sure the plug's all the way in." I made sure to be helpful in the safety department.

TERESA

I stopped halfway to the kitchen, turned and filled the doorway to the bedroom. "Will Brook Lynn be able to hear you?"

HYENA

"Only you. And even though you think you're speaking like a human, you're not. This is advanced, like electronic messengering but without the device."

TERESA

"Well, that's a relief." I put my fingers to my lips to see if my mouth was moving words through it. But I couldn't tell. Fingers or lips: both felt kind of numb. I went to the kitchen, put on the coffee, and snuck back down the hallway and peeked through the door; spied on the strange creature.

HYENA

"Hey, you behind the door. Your coffee's ready. Get it before it spills out the top and burns the hot plate it's on."

TERESA

"Smart ass." I padded down the hall, poured my coffee into my World's Greatest Mom mug, and returned. The hyena was on her back, all four legs sticking up in the air, head tipped back so she was looking at me upside down. She was lean, strong, and, in her silly position, seemed animated. "What—?"

HYENA

"What, what?" I wasn't giving her anything else until I heard the commitment. *I was so happy we were finally talking that I'd rolled about a bit and was on my back when she came in.*

TERESA

"I'm ready." I said it because I was.

Fargo. Not the Movie

I left Alaska in 2015. It was there I'd met my higher self, an inner-guide, then began to understand how strong I was. We had lots of discussions about my childhood—the good, the bad, the ugly, the absofuckinglutely terrifying, and I realized that the only reason I was home was because of my guide. In effect, my higher self had steered my inner-compass when the storms were the worst. It was eye-opening to know that I could journal more, go out for coffee, walk, and relax as part of a team effort—me, myself, and I were complete when I understood I had a guide—a higher self. I also had an imagination, therefore my guide appeared as a hyena, and I named her Story.

Alaska offered me a view from almost the top of the world, and from almost the top of my world. Alaska took me to the top of my game-so-far. I was so grateful to it. I'd made a difference, I'd learned a ton, and I'd met my higher self.

It was time to return home. Brook Lynn was in her teens. I felt pulled back to the Midwest. I secured a position in Fargo, North Dakota and found a place to live in my hometown of Detroit Lakes.

Fargo, North Dakota. Yes, the question most people ask me is the woodchipper one. Some people have even said I sound like the main character, police officer Marge Gunderson, played by Frances McDormand in the movie, Fargo.

The problem I encountered when I was working in Fargo, and I suspect I may have encountered lots of other places at that point in my career, is that I was a woman with quite a lot of policing experience—and a detective to boot. Many men didn't like to hear that. They didn't like the feel or the look of it—yet they had to fill certain requirements in terms of experienced officers, so the interview process did not reflect their biases or philosophy.

In the Fargo police department there were many inexperienced, young officers. They would have benefitted from an example of a strong and experienced officer like me—one who'd had her share of difficulties growing up, identified with many suspects, which made it easier for her to communicate and gain cooperation. But many found it a difficult visual to 'see' a senior female officer in that they'd grown up with male images. Others felt they had to go with the culture that had been shown to them as it was the only way they'd been able to survive in the system. Change would mean going against the grain.

Intellectually they struggled—why should they listen to someone who they saw as just a girl, a bossy sister, even a mother? It was disheartening because my mission was to help as many people as possible live peaceful lives, work their way out of difficult circumstances, and get past negative influences.

Management didn't appreciate my presence either; they didn't want a strong female officer with experience. After all, how would they control, put her down, dominate, or hurl sexist comments at a person as strong as me?

Their culture was one within their department that had already been set up to be unhelpful, and not just to me. Their attitudes were a collective—mostly—of old boys who banded together. One senior officer's hatred or bias was the next less senior officer's way. What I immediately noticed was many didn't want to lift a finger to get involved with other communities, to assist fellow officers, or really get their hands dirty and make a difference. It bothered me a lot. I continued to exercise my own high standards. Sadly, I was punished each time.

The officers who showed promise of wanting something different were quickly pulled into line by the keepers of the culture.

Fargo, the place I was born, brought me full circle. I was at the top of my game, my skills honed, and I was open to learning more and serving to the best of my ability. I gave it my all. And some of my colleagues did not like that.

No matter how hard I tried, what strategies I used to bring a sense of service and duty to the group I worked with, all I got back was a bunch of guys comparing dick sizes. This was the beginning of the downfall of my career: unsupportive men. And while I know that we are each responsible for our own rises and falls, sometimes there are extenuating circumstances that keep pushing and pushing a person down.

I had been promised the world in that job, and I came bearing the gift of experience and humility—I wasn't into comparing dick sizes.

Almost everyone there had less than five years… it was their first job.

I was not being utilized to my fullest.

I answered calls and insisted on participation in the career we'd all signed up for: supporting other departments, helping each other within and outside the office. All I got was crickets.

It got nasty. And it became dangerous.

No Room for Error

When Chris Dewey was shot on February 18, 2009, and died from those injuries a few months later, my view of law enforcement changed. I'd never considered it could happen to me. Not in a small town. Not in our community.

When the standoff was over, there was no debriefing about the shooting. No one talked about it. Everyone avoided talking about it. Never was I asked how I was doing or given the space to speak freely about my feelings. Our department moved on from the incident with our leader speaking to the media about how unfortunate it was and how his deputies did an outstanding job. All this on the airwaves, including a 'by the way, election time is coming up'.

The second shooting event was on February 19, 2013, when I was in Alaska. It took place just outside my jurisdiction. Though I had no direct involvement with this event, certainly not like Chris Dewey's shooting and standoff, it still shook me. I'd been working nights and heard dispatch radio it to an associated agency. I was working for the neighboring agency; the shooting happened three blocks from where I was patrolling.

After that, I started to wonder what was happening in terms of increased violence in the world—in my world. Every shift the dice were rolled, When would it be my name on the news? My daughter would be without a parent. Who would raise her? Who would be there for her? She needed her mom. She needed me alive.

Back then, I began to think about going to law school, but with the costs and the amount of time that would have to be invested—years of education—how I would do that? I read lots on other careers that were related to my core values and need to serve, and I discussed my situation with friends, hoping we could brainstorm me into a different line of work that still resembled justice, frontline-help. I kept putting on my gun and badge daily. I loved what I did. I believed in what I did.

The third occasion was June 23, 2015. A man called Ashley killed two people in the days before this. The victims were two blocks from the police department offices I worked from. This was a particularly challenging situation in my career because it crossed so many lines for me, and altered outcomes. This was the real shift to showing an individual's capacity to undermine, intimidate, and hurt another. That 'another' was me. That story is one I want to detail because it may help people recognize certain situations and relationships in their lives.

Two Murders in Two Days

Two innocent people. And a raging individual under the influence of drugs. It began on June 22, 2015, when Ashley Hunter went to the apartment of a supposed friend and stabbed his 'friend' seventy-seven times.

Unthinkable. Brutal. It didn't end there.

The day after the stabbing, Ashley used drugs all day and became paranoid. That evening, he wandered the streets, knocking on doors in a neighborhood. At one point, he knocked on the back door of a residence and, when it was answered, Ashley asked for a glass of water.

The person who opened the door was a kind individual, solid in his faith, and immediately recognized the individual was troubled. This kind man went to get the glass of water and made a call to the police.

While Ashley waited for the water, he became paranoid that the man was taking too long. He was aware his image had been on television based on the previous night's murder. He entered the kind man's home and began beating him with a hammer—blows to the back of the head. He killed him. Officers responded and arrived at a burning house. He'd set fire to the man's home, attempting to cover up the killing. After that, he took off into the night.

This is where I come in.

As fire trucks were on scene, the rest of us in law enforcement were on high alert looking for Ashley. Dispatches continued to receive calls from the public. Our sergeant had ordered our division to work together—two people per car—in case the suspect was spotted. I was riding in the passenger seat with my partner who was senior in rank to me. We were patrolling the neighborhoods in our jurisdiction when a call came into dispatch that the suspect had been spotted walking down University Drive. We were one block away.

My partner pulled into an intersection so that I could positively identify the suspect based on the police photo that was circulating. The streetlights allowed me to do this: it was Ashley Hunter. I called it in to dispatch, notifying them that Hunter was walking down the street at this point toward our squad car with his hands up. I was about to exit the vehicle and engage the suspect with my handgun drawn (as you do with any felony situation) when I was told by my colleague that I was not to exit the squad car to apprehend the suspect.

As I tried to reason with my colleague, Ashley got closer to us. I reached for the door handle again and continued to plead my case. He reminded me he had seniority. He said if I exited the vehicle, or even touched the door handle again, I would be reported for insubordination and written up for not following directions of a senior officer.

I was at a complete loss for words; my head was spinning, I could see the suspect right in front of us. Squad cars approached. They'd been listening to our radio traffic. One squad car, two squad cars, three squad cars, lights and sirens on. It was right out of a movie: officers by the handful exited their vehicles and ran to the suspect, firearms engaged. I sat on the sidelines and watched as one officer looked at me—dead square in the eyes—and threw his hands up in the air as if to say, WTF are you doing just sitting there?

Ashley Hunter was arrested without incident.

In those early morning hours, I realized I was being held captive a long way from any moral and honorable home. That night had not exampled my type of policing. I was working with a fearful person who either had some serious issues with fear, and/or only wanted to wear the badge.

The badge comes with an oath. I had been prevented from carrying out my oath.

"On my honor, I will never betray my integrity, my character, or the public trust. I will treat all individuals with dignity and respect and ensure that my actions are dedicated to ensuring the safety of my community and the preservation of human life. I will always have the courage to hold myself and others accountable for our actions. I will always maintain the highest ethical standards and uphold the values of my community and the agency I serve."

The event left me in absolute shambles.

- Honor means giving one's word as a bond and guarantee.
- Betrayal is defined as breaking faith and proving false.
- The badge is a visible symbol of the power of your office.
- Integrity is firm adherence to principles, both in private and public life.
- Character means the qualities and standards of behavior that distinguish an individual.
- The public trust is a duty imposed in faith to those we are sworn to serve.
- Accountability means that we are answerable and responsible for our actions.

- Community is the municipalities, neighborhoods, and citizens we serve.
- And the most important one… courage is having the 'heart', and the mental and the moral strength to venture, persevere, withstand, and overcome danger, difficulty, and fear.

Let's save that one for later because, whether a person has an official badge or not, they operate as a human, with responsibilities to themself, to their community, and to the world.

I came out of the situation knowing I'd had some rough treatment for being a female officer, for being invested in the community I served, but that being prevented from arresting Ashley Hunter had been a threat to my safety and to that of other officers, and the public.

Talking to him about it would not bring a solution. Nor would taking it above him. He echoed the department's attitude. He was the department's attitude.

The Shitstorm that Pushes Us to Change

What is it about February? It certainly seemed that this was the time of year for me to be involved in life-changing standoffs.

The fourth life-changing incident took place February 10, 2016. When I arrived for my shift in Fargo, I learned a neighboring agency reported an officer down; a suspect was barricaded in a house. It was a repeat of the car incident, except now everyone in the office had the fear of going on a dangerous call bug—or the too lazy to respond to an officer in need bug—though I'm not sure the word is lazy.

At that time, when the call came in, I readied to get myself to the scene and looked around. There were no high-quality values in sight; not one single partner in my agency was willing to provide help to the other agency. In that moment of refusal from them, I loaded up my squad car and immediately went to the aid of the other agency. My colleagues sat back at the office, either scared to go out to help, or due to pure lack of respect for what the blue line really meant. This was a huge awakening for me. Could this be happening? It was.

Not only that, but I was putting nails in my own coffin: damned if I did help—my fellow officers had attitude about that—and damned if I didn't because that went against my values and my oath.

Hey, I really did not want to start my shift, one minute in, like this, but when someone asks for help, then hell, yes, you go. I finished up getting my squad car ready, checking over my long gun, making sure I was prepared to enter into a scene. I thought to myself: you all want to wear the uniform and badge but don't want to work for it. It disgusted me. I also knew I was up against a bunch of men, not one. A whole bunch. Who'd believe me? Who would I go to?

I pulled out of the parking garage on a cold winter night and headed the three miles to the area of the other officers. I radioed into their department, letting them know I was in the area and waiting for instruction on where they wanted me posted. At this time, gun shots were ringing out. Officers were getting onto their police radios asking every officer to give a status of location and well-being. Everyone jumped in and accounted for themselves except one officer. Numerous radio calls to him and no answer from Jason Mozer.

A formation of officers went toward his last known location. He was lying in an alleyway, unresponsive.

It was discovered that, around seven that night, a call had come into dispatch that the caller's father had fired a gun at the caller's mother. The caller and mother were able to leave the home unharmed, but the suspect had barricaded himself in the house and had begun randomly shooting from the house to the alley and the street. One of these rounds struck officer Jason Moszer. That shot killed him.

The standoff went on throughout the night. The suspect later succumbed to a self-inflicted gunshot wound.

I could not get my mind off the scene back at the office. Fellow officers sitting there while others were risking their lives. Butts in chairs at the same time when calls are coming in for help. It was another red flag that my fellow officers would not ever be there to cover me.

I had landed back in the Midwest, a detective from Alaska, to a whole different world. A world in which a strong woman, confident in her skills, training, and secure in herself, was in the wrong department, the wrong area of the country, or maybe the wrong career. We were supposed to band together to serve and protect. I had no fight left in me to fight the good fight.

On the Job

I continued to try to make change by exampling excellent police work from within. I was buoyed and inspired by officers around the country who would stop and toss a ball around with a kid, help an old lady across the street, shovel snow from a driveway—yes, cliché but endearing and life-changing actions.

My ideas of community policing were not embraced by my peers.

I enjoyed going to work; not one single day did I say I was stressed out. The pure joy of getting into my squad car, taking on cases, looking into things, report writing the whole process brought me so much joy. Regardless of the attitude in the department, the concept of stress never occurred to me. Yes, I felt anxiety to get cases done, timelines to figure out all the pieces, but that drove me to get it done, figure it out and get a conviction for the case. Never stressed. Even when I was holding a gun pointed at a house where two suspects were holed up after shooting one of my partners, I felt empowered to get the assholes out of the house. Sure, I was tired, even exhausted at times, and I was hurt and dismayed by the attitudes. I don't think I realized how my life really was affected until about three years after my career in law enforcement. That's what made it hard to think about leaving. I loved my job I was not stressed. Frustrated with my peers at times, yes.

Politics and Sad Men

Every shift was another experience of balancing serving the community and being painted further into a corner.

The officer hell bent on making my life miserable—or anyone else who wanted to engage in real police work—continued with his dirty tricks. There was no getting through to him. He had seniority, and he used it. Sadly, he was cracking open and fighting it by trying to bring me down.

One key event was when the North Dakota Supreme Court ruled the agency I was working for did not have the authority to make arrests outside areas specific to their jurisdiction. There were turf wars; politics weighed heavily into decisions. My job was to follow the rules I was given to the letter of the law. Long story short, it came to be that certain areas close to our patrol areas were out of bounds for us to act on arrests or charges.

On my days off I received an email with new maps and jurisdiction guidelines. I studied these maps, marking them with a highlighter and writing a cheat sheet of the specific locations I was allowed to enforce laws.

On my return to work, I packed my items into my squad car, checked over my lights and my firearms, and made sure I was set up for a successful shift. I took out my new map and drove several times around the area I was allowed to patrol—did this for muscle memory.

Unbeknownst to me, the fuckery began when I spotted a vehicle with an expired registration and called it in. When the male driver pulled over, the officer who had been harassing me—and heard my call to dispatch—pulled up in a squad car at the scene.

The driver was totally cooperative but nervous. Turned out he had no insurance either.

As I went about the half hour of work to do all the necessary checking, my colleague remained beside my car, observing me. I went about helping the driver to save money by suggesting he park his vehicle instead of having it towed. Then I helped him contact someone to come pick him up.

When we wrapped it all up, I thanked my colleague for his back up, then watched him drive away. Less then ten minutes later I received a call from my sergeant who requested I report to the office.

When I arrived, my colleague—the officer who had made my life miserable for months, who had within the last hour stood beside my cruiser—was watching YouTube videos, his back to me.

My sergeant questioned me about the traffic stop. I gave her the information she requested. She stated it had been brought to her attention that this was outside our jurisdiction, and I would have to revoke the citation. I explained the location of the traffic stop was within our jurisdiction and that I was one-hundred percent sure it was a valid stop.

The problem officer sat quietly, watching his videos. I registered my blood pressure rise. I raised my voice and asked why the hell would that man—I pointed to him—my colleague who is supposed to have my back, sit on a traffic stop for half an hour and not tell me this was out of our jurisdiction?

Crickets.

I asked him to turn around and look at me. He did turn. I'm not sure he expected me to be so demanding. He appeared as a scared little boy with a confused look on his face.

I asked him, in front of our sergeant, "Tell me, why would you stand next to me on a traffic stop for thirty minutes and not tell me it was out of jurisdiction?"

Eventually, he said: "I wasn't sure at the time, so after you cleared the stop, I came up to the office to talk to the sergeant about it."

After a lengthy discussion, and the location identified on a map, I told our sergeant I would not revoke the citation. She ordered me to call the driver of the car and tell him to tear up the ticket. I obeyed her order.

When I finished speaking to the driver, my sergeant then approached me, having realized she was wrong. She had fallen for my colleague's tricks.

I began to fume and, as my 'colleague' looked at me, I called him a fucking snake and a worthless partner that could not be trusted on a traffic stop let alone in any life-or-death situation.

His retaliation kicked into high gear: making up stories, telling lies about me to anyone who would listen—he even tried it with officers who liked me and knew my work ethic and dedication. He worked hard at getting them to change their minds about me, but they just came to me and told me what he was saying.

He had perfected flying under the radar. And he supplemented his ego by picking on others. His seniority allowed for it.

The Finale

When my trouble-making colleague failed to get under my skin during work hours, he went after me with a kind of sordid and voyeuristic attack relating to my personal life. It resulted in an investigation against me, for which I was cleared.

Winter in Minnesota is cold and nasty. There was a three-day cruise—Friday to Monday—to the Bahamas. It was a super-cheap price and known as a party/booze cruise. This was not a concern to Brook Lynn and me. There would be sun and sea and that was good enough for me and for Brook Lynn who was sixteen. We treasured our time together and looked forward to a break to catch some sun and just be together.

As is the case in the Midwest, a heavy snowstorm hit; our flight was delayed hour by hour, we were exhausted on our arrival in Miami where were spending thee night before boarding the cruise the next morning.

We dropped our luggage at the hotel and, since we hadn't eaten all day, we went across the street to Bubba Gump—Brook Lynn's choice.

Along with our food, I chose a margarita with a mini beer upside down in it. Brook Lynn chose a slush that came in a plastic souvenir Bubba Gump cup that had a light-up feature.

We snapped a selfie and posted it to Facebook—the two of us holding our drinks, mine alcoholic and hers not. I captioned the post 'dinner and drinks with my mini me'. That's what I have always called her, and I still do.

A short time later, our server walked by with three glasses of water, balanced one on top of the other. Brook Lynn asked him how he did that; she had waitressed as a part time job. He told her there were slits in the top of the plastic cups so that the cups would balance on one another and gave them to her for a social media photo op. Bellies full, we headed to the hotel for bed.

The next morning, we headed to the dock.

When you board a fun cruise, you're handed a little drink, and your picture is taken with the cruise line's backdrop. My drink had alcohol, hers did not—a fruity slushy. We grabbed a glass of water each and found spots poolside and took more selfies.

The weekend was fun—I've always been so proud that Brook Lynn and I could spend time together. Before I knew it, we were back in Minnesota's winter, but I was refreshed and energized.

The next three months went on as normally as it can for a police officer.

At that time, I commuted one hour each way for work. One morning, as I pulled into my driveway after a long night shift, I received an email from my lieutenant that I was being suspended with pay for actions unbecoming of an officer.

I went into shock. I had no idea what I'd done to warrant such a thing. I had never even had a warning of any kind.

I was told to report to work the next night at seven and to turn in my gun, badge, and keys to the department until the investigation was completed. When I went in at seven, I was taken into a conference room where my lieutenant, sergeant, the Chief of Police, and other administration were sitting. They then asked if I knew why I was there, and I told them I had no clue. They showed me printouts of pictures of my daughter and myself in our bikinis, pictures of the water cups, the Bubba Gump glasses, and the cruse ship promotional picture. They stated that they had been investigating me for three months and working with other agencies since we were in international waters and believed I was allowing my daughter to drink and supplying her alcohol while in the Bahamas.

I was in shock. It was ridiculous. I wanted to laugh out loud but these people were serious.

I wondered how water, a slushy at Bubba Gump, and a slushy on the cruise ship could possibly elicit this. The people accusing me of this stated they believed there was alcohol in the cups because of the nature of the vacation break and the Facebook posts.

I asked them if they had ever been on a cruise. None of them had. I explained how it is customary to get your photo on boarding, and since we'd been on a mother and daughter break, we took all the pictures we could.

I was sent home on paid leave and told they would investigate further. I raised the point that they had already been investigating me for three months and yet had no proof of their accusations. Not only that, but it was demeaning to have been working side by side with officers, while having this investigation going on behind my back.

I was bold. I said, "You have another week to get your stories straight."

The next morning, as soon as legal businesses were open, I hired an attorney, provided him with the letters I had received, the pictures, and all the tickets for airline fare and cruise, along with receipts from Bubba Gump.

Within a day, I received a letter from the department asking me to come back the following Friday (within the week) to discuss the findings of the investigation. During this time, my attorney was already communicating with administration and looking into who started the false accusations, who had gone onto my Facebook account and brought them to the attention of higher-ups, and whether this was retaliation or gender-based prejudice by the department, and/or officer(s) at the department.

One week later, I was informed that the investigation was unfounded, My gun, badge, and keys were returned to me. I restarted night shift immediately.

However, I was given a disciplinary action and had to attend a social media class then prepare and present a power point to the whole department on proper social media etiquette. This had to be done within one year of my reinstatement.

After this incident, an email went out which explained all my cases would be handled or overseen by… guess who? Well, if you guessed the cowardly officer who had tried tirelessly to undermine me, you would be correct.

One year to make a presentation on appropriate conduct?

Can you say last straw?

Two days prior to that one-year deadline I delivered my resignation letter.

*****

Self work includes self protection. Sometimes, maybe often, we wouldn't believe that someone within our workplace would go to such lengths to manipulate a system to harm a colleague. It seems to me even more severe when it is a first responder, and colleagues literally have each other's lives in their hands.

To have our trust shaken, to be betrayed and lied about, is life changing. I chose to rise from what happened to me. Sometimes, I did used to think how I could have used the legal system to bring the abuse to a larger stage, but I know it would have resulted in my not being able to do my job efficiently.

I refused to lower my standards. My oath came first. My heart goes out to other officers who have been pulled into this mess, and who are dealing with harassment because of their strength and allegiance to the badge.

NOTE: Karma, however, has a fantastic memory and is on the side of good cops and honorable people. After I left, Karma arrived, and justice was served to this officer. The great thing was, I'd already let it go. I knew I was destined for greater things. My higher self had let me know that. While I had once thought policing was the only way to serve a community, my higher self let me know how I could truly unleash my strengths and use what I'd learned.

Hyena and Me

HYENA

"Some say the world will end in fire, some say in ice."

TERESA

Do we have to do Frost every time we speak?

HYENA

You love Frost. Was the day that bad?

TERESA

The day? How about the year?

HYENA

Frost used 'ice' as a metaphor for hatred.

TERESA

He may have been born in San Francisco, but he must have spent some time with the likes of some nasty ol' boys like the ones in the department before he wrote that poem.

HYENA

Hatred is everywhere. You just see it more where you are.

TERESA

And I've seen enough of it. And I'm tired of it. Where is the warmth? Where is the love? Where is the community? And by the way, where the hell is 'his' guide? Where is 'his' higher self? What kind of mental attitude twists something in someone's personal life—with Brook Lynn for chrissakes—and convinces the higher ups? If only his energy for manipulating and meanness could be transposed into goodness. How can some humans just miserably fail other humans?

HYENA

You did the right thing. Resigning. And I'd be right beside you if you wanted to take it further. You could you know. Ultimately, if you take on the system, you won't want to work for them anymore. Besides, there's more you're wanting to do. Teresa. You're too evolved for this.

TERESA

You got that right. You're still guiding me, right? I wish you could show me my future self.

HYENA

Let's do it.

TERESA

You mean you can? How did I not know that?

HYENA

Your future self and your higher self are tight, Teresa. How did you not know that?

TERESA

Because you never told me?

HYENA

Okay, here we go. I'm gonna ask you something, first. Trust me, okay? Don't look at me like that either. Like we've reached the end of the road. This is a horrible time for you, but endings are starts. You've been paving the way to something greater. You know it. You and I both know there's a way you can use all those skills you've used in all the calls you've been on. You know community. You inspired many young women when you were a school resource officer, then on the street—understanding what they were going through—and when you were in school, as a student, others saw your stamina, your resilience, and dedication. Your next career is part of this one. You've been training all your life for this next bit. So, even if you're, right now, feeling pretty shitty about life, knowing you've done the right thing, knowing you honored that badge every day, then even at this low-energy, feeling betrayed by others way, I'm going to ask you something.

TERESA

Go on then. Get on with it. You're just chattering away. Move on with it. I don't have much patience with you right now.

HYENA

Close your eyes. Imagine you have a captive audience right now, made up of women of all ages. Eighteen, twenty-one, thirty, forty— even your peers, women your age.

TERESA

Hey, watch it with the age thing.

HYENA

That's not my point. I'm not calling you old. Let's say there are some women in their fifties and sixties too. Age is a stage, so I'm just giving you a picture of an audience.

TERESA

Whatever. Keep ramblin'.

HYENA

You're sitting with a bunch of women, in a coffee shop or an auditorium, or you had a group on a Zoom call, or you had one… one thirty-something in a one-to-one conversation… captive. What would you tell them about moving forward in life, about resilience, strength, honor?

TERESA

It feels weird. I'm just crashed here on the bed. I want to call for a pizza. I'm wiped. You're asking too much of me. Let me get back to you tomorrow. I just wanna hear your reveal of what the future has in store for me now. That way I know I have a future. I just resigned, you know.

HYENA

Phone for a pizza. And then do the thing I asked you to do—close eyes, just say what comes naturally about moving forward in life, about resilience, strength, honor. When you're finished the pizza we will almost be there, right?

TERESA

You want me to speak to a bunch of women in a coffee shop—all who want to move forward—or just one person?

HYENA

You're stalling. You never stall when you go on a call. C'mon. Call Pizza Haven, you love their special. Good. Now, go. All the women in the world who want to move forward and are stuck. Speak to them.

TERESA

I'd tell them they have a superpower. They are shapeshifters, doers, creators.

HYENA

Well, tell them. Deliver the first few lines. I'll start it for you. My name is_____

TERESA

Okay, my speech:

My name is Teresa. I have a story. You have a story, too. And it is more valuable than you think it is.

I have a formula too:

STORY + RESILIANCE + DETERMINATION
= UNMESSWITHABLE.

The combination of those three things and all the extras that go along with them make me unmesswithable.

This formula will work for you, too. I can show you how to combine your story with the resilience and determination you've demonstrated in your life, and the strength of those things that you still have, and help you rebuild your world by understanding it then ruling it. You will be unmesswithable too.

You might have heard that nothing stops you from being successful except for yourself. That is true... partly. To be yourself it's important to meet all parts of yourself. I always knew there were principles I lived by and a value system, but I didn't always know how to latch on to them because I was putting my energy into trying to find acceptance—I wanted love and would take it at any cost without understanding what it was. We all need connection. But, it turns out, the best connections are made when we have found independence within our self, and we have recognized that we have often relied on sentimental shit in life, and we have not separated emotion from fact. We, women, make more emotional decisions than the males of our species. What I've learned, and I want to help you figure out for you, is that we need to be more like hyenas.

Many women's dreams are killed off just by fear of failure. But women are not built or programmed to fail. We are fucking fortresses. If you're stuck, right now, in a 'bad' relationship, or a shitty job, or you find yourself constantly unhappy—check in moment: are you always blaming someone else?—then listen up. Your story-so-far holds the secrets to why things are the way you say they are. Your-story-from-this-point need not be that old story. It can contain it because you will learn from it, you have been learning from it (you just don't know that yet). You have a higher power within you. I will show you how to connect with that higher power, and I will join you to be your accountability partner, your extra guide, a light to help you identify what it is you want, and to get it.

HYENA

Whoop-whoop. Bravo. More. Encore. Can you see my standing ovation?

TERESA

I'm going to guide people? Am I going to die and become what you are?

HYENA

Well, eventually you'll die, but first you're going to be what you just said in that speech.

TERESA

I don't like the word life coach, okay?

HYENA

There are lots of other words.

TERESA

I did feel it, though. I felt it. I've been doing part of this all through policing and community work, but I never could do the follow up after a call, or go back and talk to the domestic violence victim, or stop in and talk to that burned out schoolteacher who wanted to join her brothers as a stone mason—she told me she had it in her.

HYENA

Now you can do that. Your resignation freed you up to do the rest of what you have been working toward all your life. You're gonna change so many people's lives.

TERESA

Yes! Women. I want to niche. Women. I know sistership.

HYENA

Listen to you. All business-niche-ey.

TERESA

I know a lot, but I'll get certified too. With the best coaching program in the world. I already know about them. I've had this as a bit of a dream-seed in me for a while, but you knew that , right?

HYENA

Hey there, CEO of The House of Hyenas.

TERESA

What?

HYENA

Your pizza's here.

We Are a Social Species

One of the things that I began to think about when I was policing was my connection to others, and how it was really a temporary connection.

While it was rewarding to help others in my capacity as an officer, I'd rarely see what came later—if they'd found the help they needed, healed from emotional or physical injuries, or found a way to improve their lives. Where did the person go? What did they do? Did they take my advice? Did they learn from their situation? Would they have benefited from a few meetings to really go through that decision on going back to school, leaving their spouse, changing careers, starting their own business, putting boundaries in place with dysfunctional friends or family?

Occasionally, after I'd had an official interaction with someone where I'd gone the extra mile and shared some strategies for improvement, I would run into them. Those were the times I could find out how things were going, and it was always rewarding to discover they'd made positive changes.

My job as a police officer was not all about arrests and court appearances. It involved sitting with people and helping them through rough patches. It was listening to people and then sharing my perspective, based on my experiences.

I kept thinking, if I have the skills to help the most stressed people in the worst situations to look at change, then I could be a positive support for anyone who wanted help to learn and change. I considered how effective I might be with people who were outside the realm of law enforcement—people looking for an accountability partner, a cheerleader and strategist in their rough patches or transitions.

The combination of my own determination and the experiences I had in listening and helping were not wasted in law enforcement, but they were definitely underutilized. I was a living example of resilience, determination, and change. I knew what it took to succeed against all odds. Most people who want change don't have to succeed against ALL odds, just some—though those odds certainly can seem insurmountable. I knew that. I had lived it.

I was often told that I related to people in the way that inspired and informed. I began to believe this to the point that I could see my communication skills were sometimes wasted because of the traditional setup of policing, and hampered by the department I worked in.

I brought compassion and empathy to the job. Every shift. It was genuine. I saw myself in many of the people I interacted with. I earned their trust because I was trustworthy. My word was everything. In my dreams, I knew I could bring this to a new level, in the private sector, with regular people who just needed to chat about things, and then have a plan to move toward their own dreams. Over time, whether I was in uniform or civilian clothes, people approached me, then invited me to engage in brainstorming.

I started to see myself in a private practice as a guide. I took that vision further: to find a highly respected certification program in which to study, and then my own company which would offer individual and group assistance by guiding. I wanted to engage and have longer relationships to help people make permanent change. I was a police officer, there to enforce the law, protect those who cannot be protected. To a point, I was a counselor, but my hands were tied in terms of being an invested coach with those I met—usually a woman, though I did have a calendar/planner in my squad car where I started keeping track of their patterns.

I also saw that, too many times, if someone had been able to have a 'buddy' to keep them on track, success would have been attainable. In the private sector, teamwork in a sisterhood would strengthen each person because of the whole.

Peers and friends told me they felt the same way about their stuckness, as did the women I dealt with on the job. My creative side continued to imagine and develop a framework of guiding, advocating, and supporting in groupwork and individual sessions.

All of this pointed toward my future. Those seeds had been inside me all along.

A Review of Determination

Having a determined mindset improves decision-making skills. That's because the best decisions come from being independent—making decisions for oneself by oneself—while balancing that with sourcing backup for those decisions from mentors and study.

When emotions run high or low, determination helps pad the discomfort of either. Determination is an engine that is running in the background, ensuring a person can ride out temporary storms.

We must fail at things to grow, to find new ways to go through problems; we learn from what we go through. Failing invites us to invent solutions or upgrade previous ones; determination fuels this movement of self. For that reason, determination can be seen as or closely related to hope.

Determination supplies hope with muscle.

Determination is created from a whole bunch of aspects of a person's personality that combine to strengthen determination. Those things can include the support a person is willing to accept (if it is in their life), their core values which then have an effect on interactions with others and opportunities.

STORY + RESILENCE + DETERMINATION
= UNMESSWITHABLE.

The formula may have the three components, but each component is a sum of many other qualities. Dissected, it is the 'story of a person' combined with two strengths that, together, hold everything: experiences of love, joy, failure, persistence, gratitude, compassion, honesty, ethics, conduct, belief systems, and everything else that has gone into making you, you.

The formula allows us to shape our identity, understand ourselves, and then create goals (and even finding a goal can be a goal—we don't all know what our passions are unless we set off on a journey of discovery).

Determination is a huge part of the formula to becoming unmesswithable. It kicks in when we identify our 'why' for something, and then feel the strength of how important the 'why' is. If we cannot get passionate about doing something, if we don't have a reason to do something beyond a 'weak' want to, or a 'mediocre' I should, then we can't expect determination to kick in.

If what we do next determines our character,
then determination helps us do the 'next'
—provided the next has meaning.

Compassion, Empathy, Sympathy, Enabling

Within the entire unmesswithable formula there exists the necessary components to be able to align with someone's experiences, and help them through their pain. Helpers can get into some gray areas when offering a shoulder to cry on or an ear to listen. Those gray areas can include some enabling. The best way to remain healthily connected to others is to understand the areas of alignment.

Compassion

Compassion is the ability to identify with the stories of the difficult times or circumstances of others rather than judging or reacting harshly; to respond with understanding or the aim to understand. It results in feeling someone's pain and wanting to help, even if it's just to listen and acknowledge a struggle.

Yes, further along the compassionate spectrum there can be problem solving, troubleshooting, and solutions, yet the core of compassion is identifying with the feelings of another.

Compassion can be confused with empathy.

Empathy

Empathy is when the feelings of the suffering are viscerally experienced by the one who wishes to help.

When we can feel for other people, then we can also feel for ourselves or learn to practice self-compassion. When we do practice self-compassion, we can more deeply feel for others.

When a person learns about self-compassion their growth is massive. I experienced this myself. When I slowed down and had a little rest without feeling guilty, I became sharper. Beyond that, I started to make space for those internal conversations that included 'what do I want?' I began to understand that it isn't what most of us were taught to think it is. Selfish is just that: Self. To put the self first. To take care of our self so that we don't burn out. Selfish is to fill the self so that we can help others. There are lots of clichés out there: 'You can't drink from an empty well.' 'Put on your own oxygen mask first.'

I think it makes sense to say that you can't give people drinks from an empty well. If you've got nothing left inside you, you can't help others. Putting it bluntly: if you're empty, you're screwed. That's an original. But it's true. When we are selfish (in a good way) we begin to see the connection between greater things and the bigger picture than we could when we were not taking care of ourselves.

Sympathy

If we know what compassion and empathy is, then what is sympathy?

Sympathy is 'feeling sorry' for someone. It is still an 'in the moment' or 'in the event' expression of sadness and sorrow. Though sympathy does not require the connection that compassion or empathy requires, it is still important. It is symbolic of a respectful acknowledgement expressed on a card: 'my sympathy (condolences) to you family on the passing of your father.' It is a recognition. It differs from empathy because empathy is remembering how it felt when your own father passed, and considering that the person who just lost their father feels the same, then sitting with them from a place of understanding. Compassion is sitting with that person and listening to the stories of their father, hearing perhaps that they'd like to have people over to celebrate their father's life and then helping them organize a gathering.

Yes, there is crossover in expressions of caring.

When caring goes beyond caring and into the zone of unhealthy, we come across enabling behavior.

Enabling

While compassion and empathy are healthy outreach, enabling is an unhealthy action or series of actions. We've said that compassion is an action that our heart wants to take to help show support. And we know from above that empathy relates to identifying with what the person is going through.

Sometimes compassion and empathy can blur the boundaries of independence and responsibility. For example, a parent may empathize with their adult child if the adult child has lost their job… but if the parent steps in and pays their child's rent month upon month, and there comes a sense of entitlement from the adult child that the parent pay that rent, then the relationship has lapsed into enabling.

Enabling results in the person being enabled to avoid consequences because the enabler has 'taken care of things' for them. In the above example, it often weakens the spirit of the adult child because they feel less capable. In the case of an enabling parent, they too are getting a psychological reward for paying the rent. Sometimes that is control and power. It is indicative of not having established healthy boundaries.

Many times, enablers dive in and rescue people from situations—or perceive they are doing good, and helping—because it feeds something that is missing within themselves. Enabling provides a powerful set of feelings for the enabler, and depletes the enabled. It occurs because people go to great lengths to ease the pain of others, but without seeing there is an overstepping of involvement. Helping someone is always well-intentioned, but over-helping can hinder the growth of all the people involved in the enabler/enabled relationship.

Summary

Until I experienced self compassion, I wasn't able to become aware of my higher self. Self compassion brought me to recognizing there was a higher self. When I was compassionate to myself—actually listened to myself and gave myself space—I began growing a self-love within, and I didn't need external validation.

A lot of people miss meeting their higher self because they are busy pouring their love out (first) instead of going within (first). A prime example is a mother. Mothers flood their children with loving messages while they themselves are a poor example for self love. Until they are able to balance that love and give it to themselves, then their children miss out on examples.

New relationships (with lovers/partners) can be affected this way too—and eventually the lack of self-love, of being in communication with the higher self, creates a burnout in the relationship or can suffocate the one receiving all the attention.

I found the best way of being compassionate to myself was treating myself how I would a friend, and reminding myself how some of the corners I cut in self care were ways I'd never do to anyone else.

Compassion and self compassion had a lot to do with my growing confidence. I learned about human behavior in law enforcement training, but I became more competent when I had met myself and journaled or doodled my dreams and listed my accomplishments. It was then that I began to shift toward the realization that I was a pretty amazing human who could mess up because that was normal too.

Self-compassionate people experience more satisfaction in life and are motivated toward goodness. This form of self-care has been related to having better relationships, being physically healthy, and is said to reduce anxiety and depression. And here's something interesting: not only does compassion and self compassion affect determination, but it builds resilience. It is the understanding through hard times, and the coping skills used through those difficulties, that brings about more creativity in dealing with issues and allows for some light which in turn generates inner strength.

Let's say that again:

The understanding we apply to our hard times,
And the coping skills used through those times,
bring creativity in dealing with new stuff.

How do you know you're not meeting your needs fully? Take this example: We literally feed others better than we do ourselves. Take the pancake scenario. Make a batch of pancakes—the first one never works, right? What do we do? We save it for ourself, then carry on with the rest, feed everyone the lovely ones, and instead of making a final one equal to the others, we just grab that cold, messed up, first one.

Here's another one we do with our work: we finish a project and tell ourselves we'll pat ourselves on the back later because we're busy. We say, as entrepreneurs, I have to get this job out, so maybe I'll celebrate my wonderfulness on this job another time. It's hard to accept our wonderfulness, but someone hired us for our gifts, right? We do the job, we get straight to the next one. After all, there are deadlines, right? Sure, we might veg in front of a movie, and even have a treat, but do we go to a quiet place, order a coffee and a piece of cake and say, yay me? Do we say, this half hour or hour is for me and my higher self? No. If we do stop working we veg out because we're exhausted; we avoid any break that is an acknowledgement. We work until we drop then we escape into a binge watch… and then the next morning we tell ourselves we're lazy for having watched shows until the early hours of the morning.

What was really happening is that there were no healthy breaks. We didn't give ourselves a single one. We just worked until we dropped.

Be mindful of your time. Watch the shows as a celebration; make sure you're recognizing it as a celebratory action for your amazingness.

When we are kind to ourselves, we fuel our determination.

Experiences on Call

Quebec Romeo Sierra Tango

ROAD-INCIDENT-ON-ROUTE-47-FOUR-
MILES-NORTH-OF-CARLISLE-ROAD-
CALLER-REPORTS-SHE-IS-NORTH-
BOUND-AND-IS-BEING-TARGETED-BY-
ANOTHER-VEHICLE-COPY.

Determination is required when coming up against seemingly undefeatable organizations who operate with a violent agenda.

Within the Indigenous sector of North America are a great many tribes who are productive, and whose communities thrive regardless of having to deal with issues of oppression and marginalization, First Nations poverty and in-fighting. As with all people, there is a darker sub-section of those with Indigenous lines who are mostly city-based.

The Native criminal gang originated in Minneapolis in the early 1990s. Its members routinely engage in drug trafficking, assault, robbery, and murder. Membership appears to float around two-hundred; new members, including juveniles, are regularly recruited from communities with large, male, Native American populations. Association with the gang is often signified by wearing red and black clothing or sporting gang-related tattoos. According to the 2011 National Gang Threat Assessment, the Native Mob (of Minneapolis) is one of the largest and most violent American Indian gangs in the U.S. and is most active in Minnesota and Wisconsin (Justice.gov 2013).

It was because of this gang that I became involved in Minnesota's largest RICO case of 2013.

Passed in 1970, the Racketeer Influenced and Corrupt Organizations Act (RICO) is a federal law designed to combat organized crime in the United States. It allows prosecution and civil penalties for racketeering activity performed as part of an ongoing criminal enterprise. Such activity may include illegal gambling, bribery, kidnapping, murder, money laundering, counterfeiting, embezzlement, drug trafficking, slavery, and a host of other unsavory business practices (Nolo.com 2022).

To convict a defendant under RICO, the government must prove that the defendant engaged in two or more instances of racketeering activity, and that the defendant directly invested in, maintained an interest in, or participated in a criminal enterprise affecting interstate or foreign commerce. This law has been used to prosecute members of the mafia, the Hells Angels, and Operation Rescue, an anti-abortion group, among many others.

So, how does a deputy sheriff from a small county sheriff's office on Native Land get entangled with such a huge case?

Let's just say I happened upon a road rage situation that led me straight into something I never thought existed in those parts.

It was early in the evening; I was out patrolling, having just started my shift. Dispatch said there was a 9-1-1 caller reporting that she was being rammed by another vehicle. Their speeds were around seventy-miles-per-hour. The caller had reported that her car had been rammed numerous times and between those times the driver of the other vehicle had pulled up next to her and tried to push her car into the ditch. The caller had two small children in the car and another female passenger. Dispatch could hear the children screaming and crying.

I was one mile away.

It didn't long before I saw two vehicles traveling at high speed. The car in chase was swerving in and out of the oncoming traffic lane; I used my radar to capture its speed: seventy-eight in a fifty-five zone.

I notified dispatch of my findings and requested back up, then activated my emergency lights. The rear vehicle came to a stop and the other vehicle continued driving while remaining on the phone with dispatch.

I began to perform a felony stop as my partner approached to assist. When I had both parties of the vehicle outside and hand-cuffed, I received an encrypted radio call asking me to step away and take a call from the narcotics officer. When I did, he asked me to keep the suspects on scene; he'd be ten minutes at most.

When the narcotics officer arrived on scene, he questioned the suspects and gained consent to search the vehicle. The suspects were arrested on numerous charges for drugs and moving violations. I then went to the victim's house to retrieve more information.

It turned out that the victim was a protected witness in a case that I knew nothing about. She was protected because she had valuable information and firsthand knowledge to drug trafficking, murder, and money laundering.

This was how I became involved with such a case, and the first time I ever charged anyone with witness tampering.

The case was much bigger than this incident, but I had a small part in the outcome to follow.

In federal court, a jury found three members of the Native Mob street gang guilty on several charges related to the gang's criminal activity. Following a nearly two-month trial, the jury found Defendant One guilty on six counts, including racketeering; Defendant Two guilty on four counts; and Defendant Three guilty on six counts, including racketeering and attempted murder.

Stemming from the same investigation more suspects appeared at trial. In December 2012, Defendant Four pleaded guilty to shooting and killing a fellow gang member. Defendant Four also pleaded guilty to one count of murder resulting from the use and carrying of a firearm during and in relation to a crime of violence.

In his plea agreement, Defendant One admitted that on February 26, 2011, he killed a friend to prevent him from offering law enforcement information about the Native Mob's criminal activities, which were the subject of a joint federal-state investigation. Defendant One admitted that on February 26, 2011, he drove to his friend's residence in Minneapolis and then shot his friend three times.

Defendant One further admitted his use of a firearm occurred during and in relation to a conspiracy to violate federal racketeering laws.

In addition to the defendants in this case, a number of Native Mob members have been prosecuted in related cases: Defendant Five and Defendant Six were convicted in 2010 of being armed career criminals in possession of firearms; Defendant Five was convicted in 2007 of assault, methamphetamine trafficking, and possession of firearms—he received a thirty-year sentence; Defendant Seven was convicted in 2008 of drug trafficking and served his sentence; and Defendant Eight pleaded guilty to racketeering conspiracy charges—he was awaiting sentencing when I left the sheriff's office.

The small part I had in this case, and being at the right place at the right time to save this woman's life, was truly eye opening for me. Especially when the US Attorney made this speech after the trial was over: "The Native Mob has wreaked havoc on tribal and non-tribal communities across Minnesota and our region. Its member's traffic in drugs and guns, using violence, intimidation and, in some instances, murder, against those who stand in their way. This case, brought against more than two dozen Native Mob members, including its leaders, exemplifies the broad reach and effectiveness of a federal RICO prosecution, which carries penalties of up to life in prison, in attacking violent criminal organizations. This investigation took several years and the cooperation of numerous local, state, federal, and tribal law enforcement agencies. Their hard work has made our communities safer."

Uniform Victor Whiskey Xray

WOMAN-IN-LABOR-123-WEST-TRAILER-PARK-COPY.

During my earlier, greener days at the sheriff's office, I was out patrolling with my field training officer (FTO)—he was a paramedic on his days off. There was a small park that was popular for illicit activities—there were no swings there; it was meant to be an oasis of nature with its massive oaks that provided shade in the summer.

The park was a one-way loop but, toward the back, people liked to pull onto the grass then use drugs, drink alcohol, and have sexual encounters. Many a coupling was interrupted here just as it was if the people had been living in their parents' home—no privacy. Still, no one seemed to care. They went to the park for teenage flings, extra marital affairs, and various rendezvous with their lovers. It was never quiet or free of activity. It was also frequented by those with healthy pursuits as it had the perfect fishing spot on the river.

I remember we were strolling through the park, wondering what we might come upon, when a call came in from dispatch. A woman was in labor in her home on the other side of town and wasn't going to make it to the hospital. She was in her bathroom; the baby was going to be born at home.

We raced back to the car and, with lights and sirens on, we headed to her home which was a long, narrow trailer. Run-down cars were strewn about the area and none of the homes were kept up—my heart went out to how people lived.

We entered through the side porch door and heard a scream of pain from the far end of the house-trailer. "I'm back here in the bathroom," the woman called out.

We found the woman on the toilet. She was wracked with pain—no amount of breathing patterns for labor, which she clearly knew, were helping.

The bathroom was the size of a front seat of a Toyota Corolla. My partner and I had to jam ourselves in there. The woman tried to stand. I could see that the baby was crowning.

To accommodate the entire situation—and crowd—my FTO asked her to get into the bathtub. I grabbed towels and we set about getting her through the pushing process and encouraged even breathing. This went on for a while.

Just as the baby was almost out, the sheriff arrived and pushed me out of the way. I may have been a new officer, but I was a woman who had personally given birth. There I stood in the narrow hall while a ridiculously large ego was jammed in the bathroom. He'd decided his being there was the priority.

The ambulance arrived in tandem with the baby's first cries.

My field training officer wrapped the baby in towels and handed the baby to the mother.

What I loved about the call was that the mom held her humor throughout the whole process. She even said that she should have known this child would be born quickly because it was her sixth.

We all started laughing.

The darker side to this call was that, even early in my career, I could see there was a club of old boys. A network. I had been pushed out of the way. Dismissed from a duty I was handling. I filed that away, but...

A few weeks later, my partner who was my FTO, and the sheriff, were each presented with 'Stork Wings'. This is a pin received by police officers for delivering a baby. Both men had their picture in the paper, complete with an article about them delivering a baby. Not only did I not receive any Stork Wings, but I wasn't even mentioned in the piece.

I didn't need to be mentioned for doing my job. But if they were deemed worthy, then why not me?

Yankee Zulu

CALLER-REPORTING-AN-INDIVIDUAL-
ON-ROOF-OF-HIGH-SCHOOL-COPY.

It was a blisteringly cold December 24th in Minnesota. Usually, Christmas Eve would be one of our slower nights. We ran a skeleton crew—my partner, Lyle, and I were it for the entire county. We were each in separate vehicles.

I was a little bored, restless, and tired of watching the snowflakes fall from the sky—it had been snowing steadily for hours. About three in the morning dispatch engaged.

CALLER-REPORTING-AN-INDIVIDUAL-
ON-ROOF-OF-HIGH-SCHOOL-COPY.

Lyle was closer to the school; he hopped on the radio and said, "On the roof? Are you sure?"

A-PARTY-ON-THE-PHONE-STATES-HE-
CAN-SEE-A-PERSON-ON-THE-TOP-OF
-THE-HIGH-SCHOOL. COPY.

"On top of the high school?" Lyle radioed back.

CALLER-STATES-THE-INDIVIDUAL-IS-
MOVING-ABOUT-ON-THE-ROOF-AP-
PEARS-TO-BE-LOOKING-FOR-ENTRY-
POINT-TO-GET-INTO-SCHOOL-FROM-
THE-ROOF-COPY.

Lyle confirmed he was en route. I headed in that direction too. I listened to Lyle ask questions of the dispatcher to relay to the caller. Appearance, size, other details.

CALLER-SAYS-HARD-TO-TELL-BUT-APPEARS-
TO-BE-MALE-IN-RED-PARKA-COPY.

Lyle replied, "Ten-four. Three minutes out."
I chimed in that I was four minutes away.

REPORTING-PARTY-SAYS-MALE-
APPEARS-TO-HAVE-LOCATED-A-ROOF-
ENTRY-IS-CARRYING-LARGE-BLACK-
BAG-COPY.

"What side of the building is the person on?" asked Lyle.

REPORTING-PARTY-STATES-LAST-POSI-
TION-NORTH-SIDE-COPY.

"On scene," said Lyle.
"One minute out," I radioed.
"I don't see anyone on top of the building. Can you ask the reporting party if he can still see the person on the roof?" asked Lyle.
"I'm on scene," I said.

REPORTING-PARTY-STATES-HE'S-LOST-
VISUAL-COPY.

"I'll drive around and see if I can see him. I don't know how anyone could get on this roof," said Lyle.

TEN-FOUR-THAT-COPY.

"Do you have the reporting party on the phone still?" asked Lyle.

TEN-FOUR-COPY.

Ask him again if he's sure it was north side," asked Lyle.

REPORTING-PARTY-STATES-THE-MAN-
IN-RED-CARRYING-LARGE-BAG-FLEW-
INTO-THE-SKY-ON-A-SLED-PULLED-
BY-REINDEER-SHOUTING- "MERRY-
CHRISTMAS-TO-ALL-AND-TO-ALL-A-
GOOD-NIGHT"-COPY.

I was sitting with the dispatcher. "Ho, ho, ho, merry Christmas, Lyle."
Officer from agency 1: "Merry Christmas, Lyle"
Officer from agency 2: "Merry Christmas, Lyle"
Deputy 1 from another county: "Merry Christmas, Lyle"
Deputy 2 from another county: "Merry Christmas, Lyle"

MERRY-CHRISTMAS-TO-ALL-AND-TO-
ALL-A-GOOD-NIGHT.

I had hatched the plan earlier, and it had gone off perfectly.

Let's Coach

Teresa, this is the shortest question I've ever asked anyone. How do I find my higher self?

You'll be happy to hear you don't have to go on an official search. Your higher self is both waiting for you and looking for you. It's also been present many times, but you just might not have recognized it as such.

The way to find your higher self is to trust.

Your higher self is kind of a shapeshifter, highly adaptable, able to respond quickly to a crisis or decision-making time. Be it a hyena, a single point of light that travels around your body, mind, and soul, or a feeling you have to convert to something identifiable—or someone— even a group of characters representing a board of directors including your grandmother, Michelangelo, a favorite teacher, and the best boss you ever had, your higher self is there waiting patiently for your 'ready'.

Sometimes your higher self expresses themself as your future self. If you're at a workshop, or do a guided meditation online, you might be led to imagine your future self and what that future self would say to you.

To best evolve a close relationship with your higher self where you work as a team, you can do a number of things to create the right environment for your higher shelf to show.

You'll need to indulge in a little creativity, even pretend. Guides and Higher Selves love it when you express originality and play.

Being open to creativity allows space for your higher self to slide in and talk to you.

That means taking the time to create the space. It might mean doing a little more reading or journaling—or starting to do that. It might include, for you, crafting a vision board, or making a list of what you want.

Hint: if you don't know what you want, I know you can make a list of what you don't want (then take the opposite of those things). It will mean quiet time, which is one of the things we don't make for ourselves. That means phone off, closed eyes, and just quiet for even five minutes. Note: you are not failing if your head is full of interruptions for those five minutes, but the intent of creating a quiet space will be recognized by your higher self and all the systems in your body.

Gratitude

The practice of gratitude is like an open door for your higher self because it involves your higher self. Whether it is a list every day—of different things than yesterday—or a few actions each day (a thank you to someone, a kind word/text that is genuine), life changes when gratitude is a daily practice.

Nature

Just as nature helps us with every issue, spending time outdoors in awe of the earth is cathartic. No one is asking you to book a trip to some ancient forest; the ground you walk on every day is ancient—it's the Earth. Discover the beauty in the cliché: stop and smell the roses. Immerse yourself in the seasons. Adventure through the greenspaces in your town or city and, if you are close, the larger ones. Claim your space in being a part of the earth.

Know your core values

Connect with your values… note those core values—lots of lists appear online and I'll publish a list too. Then clean up your social media if it doesn't reflect those values.

Journaling

That isn't as hard as it might seem. It requires a pen and a paper. It can be a napkin. It can be the inside cardboard of a box of Fruit Loops. Just let the pen sit on the 'page' and, if nothing comes to mind, then write this: I'm not going to write about…… or this is what I recall most about being six…

Let yourself respond to prompts not react to them. If you don't want to write, make a bunch of boxes and draw in each one—even if they are stick people.

Doodle online and consider what that doodle means to you… or make it into something.

Service

Be in service. Do something for someone and do it without any expectation. When
you're done—don't' tell anyone—just consider how it made you feel. When you register what it's like to be a part of the earth that is simply in anonymous service, you can then begin to drop your expectations and replace them with intentions.

All of these are ways to attract your higher self into a full relationship with you.

Let's Coach

Teresa... How does a person address manipulative relationships? What about in family?

It's more about evaluating what can be changed, who wants to change, and re-establishing a healthy way to go about change. All of that requires process including self analysis.

Finding patterns in your life is key to change so that there are no opportunities to be involved with manipulation.

When people are not clear on their values, they will often hang around others who are similar in their 'not knowing their core beliefs'. When people are in a phase of changing to understand and clarify their values, then they often notice that the people they associate with behave, well, badly. Manipulative people, bullies, misogynists, narcissists, attach themselves to people who do not have solid boundaries.

Cutting ties in families can be difficult. However, sometimes it's necessary. Most often, though, when a person establishes boundaries, the manipulation stops—not always, but often. However, by that time, the person who has asked the questions of themselves and created boundaries notices that the manipulative person is still behaving badly around others, and so they are not someone the 'change-maker' wants to be around.

Speaking out to others in the family can help, but ultimately each person has to make their own decisions about a family member. It's much the same with friends, or even neighbors. Self care is an inside job and boundaries are personal and individual to each of us.

Allow me to stretch this further because recognizing one's values and validating one's role is so key to growth and to peace.

The ability to be taught and learn from others and the desire to want more and be more are a couple qualities that made me a great officer. There are many more qualities I have that made me a great officer. There are a lot of qualities that make me a really great person. But here's the rub: most people, including me, find it hard to talk about their good qualities. To be fair, we don't have to, we just have to operate from them. What we do, though, and I used to catch myself doing this, is focusing on my worst qualities. I could list them all in a heartbeat. It is common for us to be on a constant self-improvement journey that we think has to contain a running critique about ourselves. This means finding—even searching—for things we do wrong so that we can be improved. We do this because we are embarrassed or feel braggy when we present as filled with greatness and goodness. Certain social media can put us in that frame of mind and or keep us there. Kind of like: "I'll tell you what's wrong with me and, while I'm telling you, I'll find some more that is wrong with me." It is also a common characteristic—to speak negatively of oneself—when we have been in relationships with manipulators and narcissists.

Demonstrating your amazing qualities and celebrating them for yourself with yourself is a positive thing. Reminder: not to focus on our negatives and be embarrassed or feel 'braggy' about our good points. Some think this is being humble. But putting oneself down is not humble at all. It is destructive.

Communication skills are key to change. Listening is a big part of that. Listen to others and listen to yourself.

Let's Coach

Teresa - I've had so many restarts. Gym memberships. Diets. Workshops to kickstart motivation. If it's advertised on social media, I'm there… ever hopeful for change.

You've probably heard this before: only you can change you. That's partly true.

I'd guess that you are different than you used to be because in this question you've shown awareness that the promise-programs you've invested in haven't worked for you. But let's see what the investment was. Up front it would have been financial. Money. Money for an image that showed a perfect life. A transaction that you pay for a program that fixes your problems. The thing is, without a commitment to time, consistency, and yourself, as well as to learning, the money will not net you any kind of solution.

The start of your true change comes from within, and that involves connecting with your higher self, your guide, finding your self, and pushing through some fears, addressing some tough issues, learning about boundaries. It can involve reading books, making notes and journaling, and it might include connecting with a life-guide/coach, one-on-one, for a session or two or as many as you need to become more accountable to yourself.

There are hard truths in change. And there is life. There is no instant. There is change, over time, which begins to create 'strung together aha! moments' which then become mornings, afternoons, days, weeks, months of positive living.

Conclusion: Your House

A Whole New Take on Girl Guide

I began to wind down and, for the first time in years—maybe in my life—take time to regroup and refresh. I'd never really had a break. School while raising a child, work and raising a child, shiftwork and raising a child.

I did a deep dive into the conversation I'd had with my higher self, I wanted to know where I was at. I wanted to experience some freedom and test myself in terms of if I was going to go 'all in' with having my own business and helping others. I wanted to make sure there wasn't any misunderstanding within myself.

During this 'break' which was really a transition to coaching, I went back to school to keep my brain in shape; to feed my interest in psychology and science.

I spent time reconnecting with my hopes and dreams, listening to my higher self, and strategizing the future. I considered other careers, other paths, and returned to entrepreneurship and coaching. Though I continued to support myself and satisfy my inner-workhorse, the coaching life of 'life coaching' would not go away.

In changing the way I went about my day to day, by having a day to day, rather than a life of night shifts, I was able to expand my relationships with others.

I traveled around the country, visiting places I'd always longed to go; bought a motorhome, put it by the ocean, and I focused on studying human nature. I began to reconnect with nature and truly reflect on gratitude. I took the opportunity to support Brook Lynn in starting her own business which became an instant success through her hard work and my commitment to her. All this returned me to my gifts: helping others.

More Nexts

I don't think I realized how my life was affected by trauma until after leaving law enforcement.

Policing was my salvation. It was my 'see what I can do' from a grade four desire and spark to a 'there's no way a sixteen-year-old party-goer with a risk-filled lifestyle can be a law enforcement officer'.

The interesting thing here for all of us to remember is, we—all people—are capable of much more than we think. We let our fears and judgement get in the way of our own progress.

Women have been stereotyped as being over-emotional. That is the tip of the stereotyping iceberg; many more ridiculous qualities are assigned to women. The sad thing is, in some workplaces and in some relationships, women are brainwashed, bullied, or both, into believing those stereotypes fit.

Post law enforcement, I started to see my 'self' as a house filled with rooms. I had some serious maintenance to do in some spaces and considered renovations in other parts. Lightbulbs needed replacing, beds needed to be made, and the soft furnishings needed to be replaced.

We are each a work in progress. Each of our own houses is uniquely designed to meet our individual needs. We fall in love with ideas, and bring them home to try them out, which is a great thing as long as we're not idolizing an idea or a person and trying to be them. The world has one Lady Gaga, one Malala, one Judith who delivers your mail, and only one Beyonce. The world has one me and one you. We must not abandon our true selves based on an exaggerated admiration of another. As well, if we are advocating respectfully and become unpopular, we must not feel shamed for our ideas or run from them.

We live in a culture where people love 'us' when everything is 'good'. As long we're not making waves. There's a comfort zone for others and for ourselves that includes following all the rules, not challenging them, not suggesting improvements if it puts someone out, and not upsetting anyone even if it means we will value ourselves less in trade for keeping the peace.

Hyenas don't do that. They move forward and use their skillset to advance effectively.

Hyenas are a true blend of golden tones—their fur is filled with copper highlights of sunrise and sunset—they are savannah gold. Sistership and ownership of sistership and self-ship has all those tones as well.

Progressive people do make waves. Usually, those waves are created when relationships are already difficult and require work.

I'm in love with the idea that, when we have our inner house in order to the point that we know there is work to do, scaffolding to set up, there will be shit that goes down, but we'll be ready for it. I'm in love with knowing that, when we take our resilient and determined selves and engage with intuition and strategy, we become unmesswithable, and that each of us meets regularly at The House of Hyenas.

Me and My Hyena

HYENA

"I have been one acquainted with the night. I have walked out in rain—and back in rain." You know I love me some Frost. Finish this verse for me.

TERESA

"I have outwalked the furthest city light." Frost's words are profound. Now, what is it you want? You look kind of grouchy. Have you been walking in the rain?

HYENA

It's not about where I've been walking. It's where I've been sleeping. Now that you're married it's hard to fit at the bottom of the bed.

TERESA

I've been making plenty of time for you and you know it. We've become powerful partners. Just like some of those on the force.

HYENA

I know you miss parts of it, like the feeling that you're making a difference, but you're doing okay. Look at all that you've been studying and reading. And what you've done for Brook Lynn—she's on fire with her business. You're moving mountains.

TERESA

There's more to do.

HYENA

Breathe, come on. You've faced some challenges since you left and you've done so well, it's almost as if you have a guide.

TERESA

Shut up.

HYENA

Seriously. We're an amazing team.

TERESA

Seriously. Shut up.

HYENA

Hey, watch it. I still have feelings. Higher selves, guides, powerful mentors, inner-leaders, may be strong, but we have to rest. I wanted to let you know I think you're going a bit fast. I've noticed when you're not speeding through your tasks, you tell yourself you're being lazy. You're not. Everyone needs rest.

TERESA

I get what you're saying. I do feel lazy, or that things aren't happening enough, but I've been understanding how important it is to live a balanced life. I'm just not used to it. And I am on track to fully help others, you know, like you've helped me. I want them to find their higher selves. I want to be a stand-in for their higher power while they find it. I am taking the time to rest. You know that.

HYENA

I do. I'm proud of you. You're getting the need for balance. And, oh, by the way, don't get too comfortable.

TERESA

Why?

HYENA

You're going to write a book.

Process

I was reminded, by life, that nothing happens instantly when it is to be an education of experience that leads a person to their next career adventure. I learned that, while there are 'almost-instant-generate-a-book-in-a-few-months' programs, my story would take longer because it would be a work of love, a significant and epic investment toward my future.

In the process of writing the book, I learned even more about myself—about patience, about how powerful the written word is, and that fine balance in writing about experiences and ensuring that, while truthful, there was a level of respect congruent with the experience. I relived calls and could see the takeaways from them that I hadn't seen when I was in that timeline of my life—when I was on those calls.

The book was never based on a template, it morphed into its unique format in the first few—who am I kidding? the first ten—drafts. I wondered how any books get published because the process was long—and I know why it was long—because I still had to learn about myself, and I had to make sure that it would be a fit for readers who were ready for change. I needed time to ready myself for the book to be published and to be ready for my future as a coach and speaker.

During the process, I thought about the conversations I'd had with my higher self, including the one when I'd resigned from the force. In all of those reflections, I kept seeing myself speaking about my values. I'd bring myself back to envisioning speaking to a room of women, but also listening. Listening to other women.

I thought about the questions I'd been asked of women I'd met along the way, and I thought about the questions I might be asked.

I thought about the questions I'd ask them.

I would return to my comfortable place and let the words come, some for my book, and some for what I'd say to others. I imagined and even practiced aloud a scenario in which I spoke:

Picture this: an abandoned little girl in a tiny blue house—the last house—on a dead-end street. It is the perfect metaphor for nowhere to go. Unless... there is determination.

I cheered myself on, and then fell into episodes of criticizing myself. In each round of building my House of Hyenas, I learned more.

I did a deep dive into what empowerment meant, despite it being an overused word. And I focused on how I might invite women to be a part of their change. Again, I practiced aloud:

DARE TO GATHER AS A HYENA IN A SISTERSHIP OF CHANGE

DARE TO GATHER AS A HYENA IN A SISTERSHIP OF STRENGTH

DARE TO GATHER AS A HYENA IN A SISTERSHIP OF COURAGE

Yes, that's what I'd say to a large group. Or a small one.

And in all the things I'd say to people in future conversations with them, I'd give equal time to listening because the journey of every individual wanting change requires a listener.

I knew I could be that listener. I knew that even though people have questions for 'coaches', behind those questions are the questioners' stories. I knew that I would be able to draw their stories out of them so that they could see the patterns in their lives and then make the connections to change... and find their answers.

Hyena and Me

HYENA

"Grievances are a form of impatience." Frost said that.

TERESA

That's just part of his quote. Frost finished that line with: "Griefs are a form of patience."

HYENA

And you wanted to really get into the topic of patience for your coaching, right?

TERESA

Guiding. I really wanted to simplify it in my role as a guide.

HYENA

I feel like I'm losing my job. Now you're the guide.

TERESA

Are you kidding me? Tell me what you told me earlier about patience.

HYENA

Fine. If you insist.

On the savanna I would wait for the right moment to kill prey so that my sisterhood could eat. I was patient. It was inherent, yet I still learned more from my pack. I never wanted instant gratification because I was working in harmony with nature where I knew that there was a process I would go through.

In the Hyena species, patience is survival. We are not the scavengers that people think we are. We are hunters. Without 'patience' we would starve. We take our time to apply our methods. If we didn't, we'd run ourselves into the ground.

TERESA

I know it firsthand. Success does not arrive overnight. If it does, then it is usually short term or short lived. The simple analogy here is to think about a seed and a plant, or seeds and a garden—three words: patience, weeding, harvest.

No one is asking us to wait forever, or to suffer. Patience asks us to calm so that we can respond instead of react, so we can plan instead of jumping in without a decent amount of information. Patience wants us to enjoy the journey to our goals, and gives total power of tweaking them, resetting, learning from the journey (experience) and connecting with ourself and others along the way.

HYENA

Unlike hyenas, humans often want instant gratification. This translates to obtaining the prize in dangerous ways. They seem to forget there is a process between 'want' and 'receive'… and requires they know the difference between want and need.

In your human world, patience will allow you to:
- *Focus on your long-term goals and dreams*
- *Make rational decisions*
- *Be a better listener*
- *Hold space for others*
- *Live peacefully*

Was that succinct enough?

TERESA

That was perfect, wise guide. Gonna do my own list, okay?

- In short, patience is the skill of waiting without frustration or complaint. Practicing patience is the key to improving patience.
- Being patient with others and yourself are cut from the same bolt of patience-cloth. Both benefit your relationships with others and help maintain a healthy mindset.
- Think of an impatient person you know. Got them? Okay think about their qualities: chronically stressed, rushed, sometimes sharp, perhaps not even a good listener? Those deficits show up when patience is not present. Take the opposite of those qualities: unstressed, calm, soft, an invested listener. Which serves the mind, body, and soul better? Which cultivates healthy relationships?

Mindfulness and gratitude help an impatient person develop patience. Practicing both leads to creativity and has been shown to improve teamwork and teambuilding. That brings a sistership to a higher place, don't you think?

HYENA

You know what I think? I think you're getting this bigtime.

Full Circle

I was a first responder for a long time. I still am, but now I respond to myself first. I do so with a different kind of urgency. The priority to respond to myself begins with self compassion.

I was adrift for a bit when I left law enforcement, even though I knew in my heart I was destined for extending the community service and advocating that I provided on the job.

I needed that time to rest, to restore my aching soul, to recognize the trauma I'd been through that would always be a part of me, and to decide how that trauma could be reframed to be of service to me... and then to you.

STORY + RESILIENCE + DETERMINATION has allowed me to become Unmesswithable. I rule my own world. My self-leadership is sometimes challenged by old stories, and I combat those challenges by going deep and composing new stories. I go to the quiet—and trust my intuition—and I strategize from a calm place.

That is what I want for you.

I want you to see your potential to be as strong as fuck, yet gentle to yourself.

Sisters who embody leadership measure progress by inner peace. They engage with their intuition, review their story, and create new strategy, They establish rituals to help them heal from past injuries. They emerge into a new truth of self; a life they wholly own.

Acknowledgements

Melissa Schultz-Geray

There are calls in this book that speak of dispatch. Here is the acknowledgement to the person behind those 'Dispatch to: 912' calls. Melissa was my nighthawk—she kept me alive. Close friends now, her most amazing qualities are: her dancing and singing skills to Prince at 2:00 a.m. She made the job of policing tolerable, taking off the sharp edges. She was the mothership of the sheriff's office and ran the night shift. She alerted every officer to all possible outcomes, gave fantastic and accurate directions, and simply excelled. Thorough communication. Lots of people are alive because of her, including me.

Mike Beckner

Encourager to think outside the box and grow my skills as a detective; he was uplifting, positive. An officer, detective, lieutenant, chief of police, his hard-working ethic, noble stance, straight-to-facts personality, are just a start to the many amazing qualities he exampled: honesty, loyalty, integrity, empathy, and caring toward others. He pushed people to be the best—and was selfless in doing so. During the writing of this book, he touched my heart when he said, "Stop writing this book and come back and work as a police officer." His pride in me makes me emotional.

Randi Noggle

My night nanny for so many years. Caring, selfless, always there to support me and Brook Lynn, she was a pillar in Brook Lynn's life and mine Without her I would not have been able to work the job with the peace of mind that she gave me. We are still in touch… she's not just a nanny but a lifelong friend.

Janeice Jacobson-Potthoff

My ride or die sister. We met when I was fifteen. She's been there through everything. When I needed a place to stay, she provided. When I needed a few dollars… well, I still owe her twenty dollars. Without her I wouldn't know what true friendship was. She brings a level of understanding and love to the world that is exemplary. She's the 'understander'…; the person you call if you need to bury a body.

Mom: Carol Collins, In memoriam

A baby hatch or baby box is a place where people (typically mothers) can bring babies, usually newborn, and leave them anonymously in that safe place to be found and cared for. Mom was that person who opened that box; she was on the other side ready to make sure that baby had a home. She had her way of loving, and taught me how everyone comes into another's life for a reason. Her bond with Brook Lynn was magical.

Dad: Gary Collins

The meat and potatoes kind of guy with practical solutions, who has grown into an amazing father who checks in on me and is generally interested in my life and what I'm doing. He has used Brook Lynn as his second chance. They go out to dinner, he invites her to dinner at his favorite place, Pizza Ranch. He has a renewed relationship with me through Brook Lynn… he does the dad things with her: supports her business and encourages her. Dad, I'll never get tired of saying, "Oh my god you're being just like a grandpa." Your involvement is an evolution.

Mom and Dad

I looked up to their relationship of more than fifty years. There was simply loyalty and strength through all the things they went through. I idolize that type of relationship and really respect their 'coupleship' and the always being there for each other. It never wavered … I hold on to that now for myself… they set the bar high.

Marie Beswick-Arthur

Thank you for sharing your gifts of writing, time and mentorship (basically, your brain) with me. Thank you for your patience, understanding, and your brilliant skills while writing this book. You helped take some of my lifelong stories in my head and turn them into a work of written art. This experience has been both internally challenging and rewarding; without you this wouldn't have been as great. I'm honored to say you are not just my editor but a lifelong friend—we created a sisterhood and, together, we are unmesswithable.

Richard Beswick-Arthur

I've always known you were in the background. I deeply appreciate your care and time when proofreading all the rewrites, giving ideas when I've changed my mind hundreds of times, and keeping Marie fed during our long Zoom calls. None of that went unnoticed.

Jessica Bell Design

The greatest cover designer I could ever imagine. The process with you has been seamless, creative, and most important: empowering. Thank you for turning my vision into reality.

Travis Tretbar

The person I fight life's storms with and my travel partner. Thank you for your patience and willingness to listen during the process of this incredible journey. There is a powerful steadiness in your support which I deeply appreciate it.

Ruby and Flo

My four-legged friends who have been by my side through every word written, who's antics filled the breaks and spaces between writing. Thank you for patiently listening to every draft and using your tail as a meter of how great each draft was. You're my source of unconditional love and support.

… and
Brook Lynn
I started this book with a dedication to you and I end it by honoring you.
Without you none of this would have happened.
You are the catalyst.
You are the better version of me.

About the Author

Former detective, Teresa Tretbar Collins, is a self-development and wellness coach, and the creator of a formula that works to reset the future of women who want positive change. STORY + RESILIENCE + DETERMINATION = UNMESSWITH-ABLE. Her uniquely formatted memoir and self-growth book, *The House of Hyenas*, combines her 'against all odds' birth to a teenage mom, her own teen pregnancy, further education, and a career in law enforcement, *with* real-life questions and practical answers, higher-self narratives, and police calls she attended that reflect community issues. An active support in her daughter's personal and professional life, Teresa has merged her coaching career with her love of travel. At any given time she is on the road or on location with her two Great Danes, Ruby and Flo, and can always be found online at https://www.HouseofHyenas.com and on social media platforms @houseofhyenas

Check out more from House of Hyenas